T0209193

When a Butterfly Speaks... Whispered Life Lessons

111 True Stories of Magical Monarch Moments Blending Science and Spirituality

Barbara J. Hacking

BALBOA.
PRESS
A DIVISION OF HAY HOUSE

Scripture quotations are taken from the King James Version of the Bible.

Balboa Press books may be ordered through booksellers or by contacting:

Balboa Press
A Division of Hay House
1663 Liberty Drive
Bloomington, IN 47403
www.balboapress.com
1 (877) 407-4847

Because of the dynamic nature of the Internet, any web addresses or links contained in this book may have changed since publication and may no longer be valid. The views expressed in this work are solely those of the author and do not necessarily reflect the views of the publisher, and the publisher hereby disclaims any responsibility for them.

The author of this book does not dispense medical advice or prescribe the use of any technique as a form of treatment for physical, emotional, or medical problems without the advice of a physician, either directly or indirectly. The intent of the author is only to offer information of a general nature to help you in your quest for emotional and spiritual well-being. In the event you use any of the information in this book for yourself, which is your constitutional right, the author and the publisher assume no responsibility for your actions.

Any people depicted in stock imagery provided by Getty Images are models, and such images are being used for illustrative purposes only.
Certain stock imagery © Getty Images.

Print information available on the last page.

ISBN: 978-1-9822-1201-8 (sc)
ISBN: 978-1-9822-1203-2 (hc)
ISBN: 978-1-9822-1202-5 (e)

Library of Congress Control Number: 2018910848

Balboa Press rev. date: 09/19/2018

Table of Contents

Acknowledgements

A huge thank you goes to my family! Mark, it just seems like yesterday when you found that chubby Monarch caterpillar on Blue Mountain, when we were newly married. You shared your love of nature with me and it was contagious! Since that moment, we have journeyed together through these days called life and have had many exciting Monarch memories, especially with our children Ryan and Rachel. Butterflies have touched our lives in so many ways, bringing us together as a family, as we witnessed the miraculous metamorphosis of a butterfly. We learned to respect nature and appreciate all the gifts it has to offer. What we respect and appreciate, we protect!

Thank you to the butterflies who keep presenting me with life lessons over and over again until I get them right! I can't imagine life without them in it….and I hope I never have to! They truly inspire me.

Thank you to my students who enthusiastically responded to having Monarchs in the classroom. Your curiosity demonstrated the key to true learning. I have learned so much from you!!

Thanks to Ev Scott for the reminders that I needed to write a book and modelling how to do that! Your encouragement has meant a lot!

Thanks to Dee Leifso for the equipment and push that I needed. I once gifted you with a butterfly and you gifted me with this journal.

Thank you to my husband, Mark Hacking and Angela Gerretsen who helped edit this book. If you find any errors, you can blame them. LOL!

Thank you to all the people who have come into my life and enhanced it, oh so greatly because of our mutual passion for butterflies. I have learned so much and continue to do so. A special thank you goes to Mike Ward for helping me expand my knowledge of other butterfly species as well as pollinator plants.

Thank you to the people who have allowed me to share their amazing Monarch stories. May they inspire others to believe in Monarch magic.

Thank you to Ted Blowes, who was my mentor, for what retirement should look like. Unfortunately, he left this Earth far too soon, with work still left to be done. I shared my passion for butterflies with him and he helped me to realize this passion was a gift to treasure and share with the world. I know that Ted is still acting as a mentor and guiding many of my actions.

Thank you to Luc Picard who became my inspirational guide on the magical Monarch mountains. You remind me of the wisdom of the universe and how to surrender to it.

I am grateful to my wise parents who taught me the importance of family and to follow my passion. My Dad, a high school guidance counsellor by day, a gardener and poet during his free time and to my Mom, a primary school teacher, who baked the very best banana muffins.They were such great role models of how to live a simple, happy life. How lucky I was to be their daughter!

Finally, thank you to the creator of all life. This truly is a magnificent world, filled with mystery, wonder and miracles.

Welcome to My World;
The World of Butterflies

March 29, 2017

This journal documents the many ways Monarch butterflies have touched my life and the many lessons and people that have come my way because of our connection. Teaching and learning with the Monarchs each fall, in the classroom, transformed my life in so many ways. I am grateful beyond measure.

I was constantly amazed as this book was being written. In fact, it felt like it was writing itself! The stories continued to flow from my memory bank to the paper. It was as if a butterfly was sitting on my shoulder, whispering what words of wisdom needed to be blended together. When I finished the first journal, I felt like that could be the end… but I was in the middle of a story and started a second journal. The stories continued to flow.

I decided to keep the writing as a journal and in the order the stories were written. Some information may be repeated, but that is so each story could stand on its own. Some names have been withheld to ensure anonymity.

For now, the writing is done, although I'm sure there will be many more times a butterfly speaks to me, and in many interesting ways..

May 6, 2018

I was right!

I am still writing this book...and I'm not complaining. The stories continue to flow. I do know however, that I had better finish soon, otherwise the Monarchs will be here again with more messages, creating more stories.

Initially, the journal was written from past memories. As the book continues to metamorphosize, it is being written as events occur.

June 8, 2018

My wise friend, Luc, gave me some excellent advice. He said I'm not to stop writing; just stop the book and switch to a new journal. So that's what I did.

When the Writer is Ready, the Tools Appear

February 1, 2017

From many different directions, I am being reminded that there are stories within me that need to flow on to the pages of this book. I guess winning this journal as a door prize last night was my clue that the time had come. No more excuses. No more stalling. Coincidentally, it was also the twelfth anniversary of my Dad's passing. He was an avid writer/poet until he turned 85. He decided then, he would write no more "odes" which he was famous for, with all who had the pleasure of knowing him. My Dad was always building people up, with the poems he wrote for them. It was at that time my young daughter, Rachel and I mysteriously became writers. Poetry, stories and songs began to materialize out of nowhere. It was like someone else was writing and we were the channels that were selected to get them down on paper.

Soon life took over, and the writing became less frequent.

When I retired from teaching almost 5 years ago, I planned to have more time for reading and writing but that was not to be. At least not yet. It was a time for traveling, destressing, and becoming better acquainted with the wonderful community, and world I live in.

From the many stories that circle within me, what would be the first book to be written?

Why Write About Monarch Butterflies?

February 1, 2017

Although I have started to write about the adventures of Harrison, the traveling Teddy bear, who brought many tales of the world back to my classroom, I feel that needs to sit on the back burner... at least for now. My deep love and appreciation for Monarch butterflies and other pollinators seems to be bubbling up to the surface at the present time... why?

Monarch populations are declining. They need and deserve our protection....and they need it now!

Butterflies have taught me many important life lessons which I am most grateful for.

Butterflies visit when I need them the most.

The people I have been led to because of this passion have made life exciting and interesting.

Monarchs have helped me see the miracles that exist in nature and I feel the need to preserve what we have. Our children and their children deserve to experience these wonders of the world.

They are a common interest Mark and I share, and they have helped create a strong bond that holds our marriage together. Time spent in nature is quality time.

Observing the metamorphosis of a Monarch butterfly was one of the greatest and most exciting moments we had the privilege of sharing with our own children. As a primary teacher, I loved beginning a new school year, each September, with the magical teaching moments the Monarchs created.

Monarchs remind us that Mexico, the United States and Canada must work together to preserve their existence and ultimately our own. Their miraculous migration depends on all three countries. No walls are necessary. Donald Trump, in his first week as President announced a wall would be built between the United States and Mexico. Luckily, being Mexican mountain dwellers during the winter months, the Monarchs would be able to fly over it easily as they migrate in both directions!

Butterflies are peaceful creatures and we as humans need to follow their fine example.

They, just plain and simple, make me feel awesome!

Watching them! Releasing them! Planting for them! Sharing them!

A Butterfly in January

February 1, 2017

Since yesterday was the twelfth anniversary of my dear Dad's passing, it only seems fitting that I start my butterfly book with what happened on that day, many years ago.

As I entered my parents' house to make funeral arrangements, I couldn't help but hear the Cardinal that was happily singing in a naked tree, in the park across the street. I turned to see this cheery visitor wearing his bright, red coat. My brothers had seen him before me, when they arrived, so he had been there for quite some time, singing his little heart out, begging for our attention. Cardinals are often seen as a messenger when someone who has passed away is close. I loved seeing this Cardinal, but secretly wished I would see a butterfly. I knew that was an impossibility on this final day of January, at least in this part of the world!

As I drove home that evening, I was in awe as the sun began to set along the country roads I traveled on. To my surprise, the sunset transformed into the shape of a butterfly. I drove into the sunset with happy tears streaming down my cheeks until I could see it no longer. I had received my butterfly after all. I sure wish I had my camera! I guess I was meant to just enjoy the moment. No distractions!

It's heavenly presence will be forever etched in my mind. Our mind becomes the camera as special images are permanently captured in our memory banks. We can return to these images at any given moment, and I often do.

A few weeks later, I was on my way to Mexico for my first visit to the overwintering grounds of the Monarchs. I traveled to the mountains with the Monarch Teacher Network, beside other Canadian and American teachers. I couldn't help but feel my Dad had been inside a chrysalis during the last few months of his life, as his body began to no longer do what it had done, for the past ninety years. I remember sitting at the top of Cerro Pelon mountain, in a snowstorm of butterflies, feeling that my Dad's spirit was there with me. He was now free to fly, no longer weighed down by his aging body.

Connections

February 1, 2017

Five years later, my dear Mom passed away just before Christmas in her 94th year. In fact, her funeral was Christmas Eve! Again, I longed for a sign that she was okay. Butterflies at Christmas, in Canada, just weren't going to appear. When I woke up Christmas morning, the sun was streaming in the bedroom window, illuminating my parents' photo. I was reminded that they were together again after four Christmases apart and that truly was the gift I needed to get me through that day.

The following May, our family went to Fern Resort where my parents had spent their honeymoon 66 years earlier. They had generously treated the entire family to a long weekend each Victoria Day. We were a family of teachers and really appreciated this downtime before facing report cards and other year end activities. Special memories were created and we enjoyed being together as a family. Each year we marveled at how much the kids had grown since the previous year. This was an exceptionally hard visit as it was the first time without my parents and it was so noticeably different.

The first night there, I had the most vivid dream that my parents were walking towards me, hand in hand. They were smiling and looked young again, as if the years had melted away. I awoke feeling elated with happiness and a sense of peace.

That day I was out for a walk and noticed a Giant Swallowtail butterfly following me. Was I imagining things? When I walked, it moved with me. When I stopped, it stopped too. Mark came along and the butterfly disappeared. When he went away, miraculously the butterfly returned. This time it landed at my feet and I was able to get its photo. It was obviously trying to get my attention.

It wasn't until I got home and viewed it on the large computer screen, that I discovered my Mom's initials (D. E.) were created by the black scales on the yellow wings. Each time I see a Giant Swallowtail now, I am reminded of my dear Mom, as they all seem to exhibit similar markings among their scales.

So sometimes the signs we ask for may not come right away, but if you ask for them, they will come.

June 1, 2018

Today I received the most uplifting message from my childhood friend who now lives in Scotland.

"Hi. Saw psychic medium. Asked about a Rachel, Barbara and a butterfly tree. Said Dorothy was there and very proud, hands sending butterflies to Barb. No prompting from me. Amazing !!!"

Rachel, my daughter and I recently took a trip to Macheros, Mexico to spend a week visiting the overwintering grounds of the Monarch butterflies. We were greeted with many gorgeous trees just covered with Monarchs. It was breathtaking!

The last time I went to a medium, she told me that my Mom was surrounded by flying butterflies. Today she was sending them to me. Such a comforting and beautiful message to receive! It reaffirms for me that there is life beyond this physical world and one day we will reunite with those we love.

June 19, 2018

Today, my friend Lorie in Colorado sent me this beautiful message. What a thoughtful thing to do. It really made my day. Even that Giant Swallowtail has my Mom's initials. Look carefully!

These guys always make me think of you So, just know you're thought of often!

June 21, 2018

Today, a sweet friend sent this quote because she knew I was working on a butterfly book. "Butterflies cannot see their wings. But the rest of the world can. You are beautiful and while you may not see it, we can."

How lovely for these people to take the time to send a note just to let someone know that they are thinking about them, or what they are doing. With social media, we can do this often and easily and you can really make someone's day. You never know when kind words can turn someone's day around. My dear Mother didn't have social media, but she often took the time to connect with people and lift them up. Even now she finds ways to do that!

Memories

February 5, 2017

Sunday mornings always seem to be a time when I am drawn to pick up my journal and write.

Today, the angel card I drew was "Memories". It reminded me that much can be accomplished by revisiting cherished memories. So I guess that's what I am doing by getting these experiences captured permanently in this journal. These stories aren't about living in the past, they are about learning from it.

There are memories of life events that stick with us, as we live each moment leading to our future. I am constantly amazed how butterflies and sometimes other winged friends find their way into my life at these times.

Retirement

February 5, 2017

As I cleared out my classroom on the very last school day for me in June, 2012, I realized I was saying goodbye to what was a very big part of my life for the last 30 years. I was grateful to my good friend and colleague, Kim, who came to help me face this overwhelming task. As we reminisced, we realized that our careers had passed by, in the blink of an eye.

How lucky I was to spend my days in a primary classroom with 6 to 8-year-olds who taught me so much more than I could ever teach them. Their excitement for learning, especially about nature, was contagious and I can honestly say I never watched the clock. The days, the months and the years passed by so quickly.

When I was finished in my classroom, it was 7:11 p.m. and everyone else had left to enjoy the summer. I no longer had to hurry. The rest of my life was waiting for me. I picked up a stone that my friend, another Kim, had given me that said "Peace". I wondered if I would ever find that peace, as I transitioned into this new stage of my life.

I slowly looked around as I walked down the corridor of the school for the last time as a member of the staff. This hallway held so many memories, but it was time to bravely go through the doors and leave my career behind.

As I left the school, a Monarch butterfly danced over my head and beckoned me to follow her to the pollinator garden that I had been guided to create a few years earlier. It was as if she had been waiting for me to finally finish the tasks I needed to complete, before drawing the curtains on my formal teaching days. She knew that my life as a teacher was not yet over; it was just metamorphosing into something different.

My parents, who were both teachers used to say to me when I left for Teachers' College, "You will spend the next year learning how to be a teacher and the rest of your life trying to forget". I chuckled as their words came back to me.

Many lessons had been taught in this garden. So many memories of children discovering the secrets of nature!

I paused at the metal butterfly my colleague, Kate, had so kindly placed in the garden during my last few days as a teacher. It touched my heart in ways I never knew were possible.

The gazebo archway was adorned with a wrought iron butterfly. It had been placed there when my mother passed away by my kind and caring staff. It had always given me comfort when I looked out my classroom window, which overlooked the butterfly garden.

The song that had been played the day before at our final school assembly ran through my mind. These particular lyrics really spoke to me at this moment, "Bless the butterfly, give her the strength to fly".

Many butterflies had been released here in this butterfly garden to continue their miraculous journey. It was time for me to continue mine.

I had never noticed how beautiful clouds can be. Is it possible that I never looked up when I was teaching? I think the following quote by W. B. Yeats says it all. "The world is full of magic things, patiently waiting for our senses to grow sharper." My senses grew sharper that day!

Although it was the end of June and still pretty early to see Monarchs in the garden, I was amazed, but not entirely surprised to find that this magical Monarch had led me to seven, fully grown Monarch caterpillars, munching on the purposely planted milkweed. I picked one up and lovingly carried it home. I made up my mind that I would grieve the loss of this part of my life, only until this new friend had turned into its adult form. Then, I would release it with joy as I celebrated my new found freedom. It was up to me now!

The gold butterfly ring my staff had given me, reminded me how lucky I was to share my life with so many wonderful children and fellow educators.

This was not the first time Monarchs had come to celebrate retirement at our school. A few years earlier I had two Monarch chrysalids that eclosed (emerged) on the first day of summer holidays. It was also the first day of retirement for Ruth and Joyce, two of my wonderful colleagues. They too, released their butterflies with joy as they embraced retirement from the career they had dedicated their lives to. I didn't usually have Monarch caterpillars in my classroom during the month of June... but I did that year.

One of my dreams when I retired was to visit Point Pelee National Park in September, during the Monarchs' migration season. Each autumn, many of the Monarchs roost in the trees lining the coast of Canada's most southern tip, waiting for just the right conditions to cross Lake Erie. It was not to be, at least not this year. There weren't enough Monarchs to even do an official count. Mark, only found one caterpillar that fall and if he can't find them, they aren't there! We had teachers calling us for caterpillars for their classrooms and we had nothing to give them. The official count in Mexico was dangerously low. My new dream now was to see them make a miraculous comeback.

When a Butterfly Speaks.

February 7, 2017 (6:00 a.m.)

As my mind was returning from the land of dreams, these words started to dance in my head, until I finally was convinced to get up and write them down before they were lost forever.

When a butterfly speaks... you must listen carefully for they are full of wisdom and their messages are profound.

When a butterfly speaks...not everyone can hear.

When a butterfly speaks...the rest of the world pauses and it's just you and the butterfly.

When a butterfly speaks...one must truly listen, watch with their inner eyes and feel with their heart.

When a butterfly speaks...it's miraculous; magically, they communicate without words.

I guess, they have been speaking to me for years, and I am now just beginning to listen.

How It All Got Started

February 22, 2017

Today, my friends Alla and Effie, came into the boutique where I was working and asked me how my butterfly passion got started. Perhaps obsession is a better word! That was a very good question, because I'm not really sure.

When I was very young, but old enough to remember, I was gifted with a beautifully framed picture of a Victorian couple dancing. The skirt of the lady's dress came alive with the iridescent colours of Blue Morpho butterfly wings. It was the most exquisite thing I had ever seen.

The two elderly sisters who lived on our block were so kind to give it to someone so young, for it easily could have been destroyed by a child who didn't understand the meaning of the words, delicate or fragile. I always treasured it and still do. It was created in the year 1924 and now stands behind glass doors and is one of my most valued possessions. Even though it is almost one hundred years later, the colours are just as vibrant as they were when I first received it.

Perhaps, the Palmer girls had given me much more, with this heartfelt gift!

When I was sixteen, I became mesmerized by the butterfly symbol. Butterfly earrings! Butterfly-etched wooden clogs! Butterflies embroidered on my jeans. It was the seventies! Butterflies on everything! Perhaps it was a hint that my life was about to be transformed… and it was! That's when I started dating my future husband, Mark.

Dee's Gift to Me

February 5, 2017 (6:18 a.m.)

I gifted Dee with a butterfly and she gifted me with this journal…

The words are flowing and flowing quickly…

For a long time, I've known that I needed to write this book. I knew I had been chosen for some mystical reason. As true experiences danced in my memories, I knew one day they would find their way into written form. I thought the time might be right, when I go to the Mexican Monarch mountains, but there are 17 days before I will be there. I thought, maybe I would find the writer within me in my magical place, but it was meant to be earlier.

About a month ago, just before I was gifted with this journal, I came across a saying, "Never force anything. For if it's meant to be, it will be." It really resonated with me and I put it as my Facebook cover photo. I guess I would be ready to write this book when it was ready to be written, and not before. Little did I know it would be soon.

18

We Are Not Getting Older; Just Better!

February 5, 2017

I've often said if it was possible to go back in time and be young once again, I wouldn't. There is something to be said for the wealth of knowledge that comes with age. If I could go back in time knowing what I know now, and take the lessons I have learned with me, that might be a different story.

I don't think a butterfly would choose to go back in time because they just keep getting more beautiful. We do too, although we sometimes don't see aging as a positive thing. They enjoy each stage along the way until they are free to fly. We should too! As the old saying goes, "Never feel bad about getting older.

It's a privilege denied to many."

If the tattered wings of a butterfly could speak… what stories would they tell of days gone by, places visited and lives touched?

Imagination

February 5, 2017

I once posted a photo on Facebook of what I thought looked like a butterfly-shaped cloud and I was told by a well-respected friend that I had a fantastic imagination. I guess he didn't see it the same way I did… and that's perfectly fine.

I often see butterflies where other people don't; the cute little brown patch on my cat's nose (even though Angel has been in our house for 14 years, I just noticed the white butterfly moustache she adorns as well, while getting the photos ready for this book), on tiny plants growing in the garden or forest and even strawberries.

After spending a glorious week in Macheros, Mexico with the Monarch butterflies, I went for a walk the day after I returned. I was amused to see that the squirrels had left butterfly-shaped pawprints for me in the snow. They were everywhere! I thought I was dreaming.

Last fall, when out for a walk, I thought I saw butterflies dancing around a tree. It turns out they were just coloured leaves swirling in the autumn breeze until they came to rest on the ground below. I took a video because it was unbelievable how much they looked like the butterflies I had witnessed on the Mexican mountains. Many of my friends thought so too, or perhaps they were just humouring me.

And if you hang around me, don't be surprised if you start imagining butterflies too. One day I opened our back door and there was a gorgeous rainbow. I had a seven year old friend with me and she thought she could see a butterfly cloud beside it. I was thinking the same thing but hadn't said anything. Maybe I'm not so crazy after all!

May 14, 2018

Today, Mark and I went hiking on the trails at Mono Cliffs Provincial Park. My imagination was running wild! It must be remnants of being a primary school teacher! I had a tiny, white butterfly kiss my finger and saw many of the early spring flowers imitating butterflies. To top it off, we saw a red-belted bumblebee and it looked like it had a yellow butterfly riding on its back. Its fuzzy markings were exquisite. Imagination is a wonderful thing, especially when walking in nature.

May 29, 2018

"Treasure your greatest gift—your imagination."

Dr. Wayne W. Dyer in his book Wishes Fulfilled

July 11, 2018

Although I thought I had completed this book, I felt the need to squeeze in this touching story and it seems to fit here.

My friend, Cindy and I met at The Ted Blowes Memorial Pollinator Peace Garden today, to release a beautiful Swallowtail butterfly in memory of her late husband. It has been seven years since he left this Earth after fighting his battle with cancer, at the age of 54.

After I handed her the butterfly, she walked about the garden searching for the perfect place to release the flying gem. A beautiful yellow bird sat among the gorgeous flowers and watched us. There were many other pollinators dancing around in the Sun's rays. So much emotion flooded up inside of her as she chose the top of the tranquil waterfall. She felt the sadness of this great loss, not only for herself but for their children. She asked him for strength to keep moving forward. The butterfly wasn't quite ready to fly, so it was placed on her heart. Before long, it's job was done. It was up and away toward the nearby trees.

We paused at the pollinator garden and noticed a heart-shaped cloud in the azure blue sky. Cindy noted there was a hole in the heart, as if it was broken. As we watched, the hole in the heart mended before our very eyes and in seconds, the cloud transformed into something totally different. Cindy and I looked at each other in amazement and smiled. We then saw an additional heart-shaped cloud, only smaller. It was as if the clouds were putting on a show, just for us. When we looked over our shoulder, we noticed what else Mother Nature had created. There was a butterfly-shaped cloud. It was incredible!... and unbelievable, at the same time. The cloud artists were working overtime today!

When Cindy got home, she texted me that there was a butterfly waiting for her on her side door. It just sat there. It did not move or fly away! Remarkable!

Imagination?

The Symbolic Meaning of Butterflies

February 7, 2017

Since the words are starting to materialize, I decided to go to a workshop called "Positive Pens" masterminded by Andrea Eygenraam. I saw it on Facebook this morning and it's on tonight, so why not? It has been said that "when the student is ready, the teacher appears".

I heard Andrea speak in January and I love her style. So positive and honest. She also has the same butterfly as me on her business cards. A coincidence? Perhaps…

Within five minutes of sitting down at the workshop, we were discussing butterflies. Again, I was not surprised to see four beautifully coloured butterfly tattoos sitting on Andrea's shoulder.

Butterflies represent many things to many people. Their metamorphosis is intriguing and symbolic of transitions from one stage to another.

From life into death.
From near death (suicidal thoughts/illness) into life.
From working into retirement.
From being single to being married.
From being married to being single.
From being childless to being a parent.
From being a parent to having an empty nest…

Life is full of transformation. The key is to adapt to these transitions as easily as possible. The butterfly reminds us that we are a work in progress, constantly changing and change is a part of life. Look how beautifully it adapts from one stage to the next.

It goes from munching on its eggshell, to chewing on milkweed leaves, to not eating for up to two weeks while in its chrysalis and then its mouthpiece totally transforms into a straw-like proboscis suitable for sucking up nectar.

It goes from being confined to a small space in its eggshell, to being free to explore with its many legs, to shedding those legs and becoming chrysalis-bound until it emerges back into the world, able to walk once again, as well as free to fly wherever life takes it.

The changes a butterfly goes through are so incredible; but then again, take a moment to reflect on the changes we as humans go through in our lifetime. They are so slow and steady over time, that we may not even notice, but they are just as amazing.

Janet and Bill's Butterfly

February 7, 2017

Over the years, many of the butterflies we have raised have found their way, miraculously, to people who needed comforting at a time of great loss. The following story started at the beginning of one school year and was in the making until the very last school day. It is still vivid in the minds of those who experienced it!

Janet Jamison arrived at Avon school, ready to take on her new role as principal. Her husband, Bill, came to see where his wife would be spending her days and he eagerly toured the school's butterfly gardens. His keen eyes discovered a Swallowtail caterpillar happily munching on the Rue plant.

It soon became part of the science lessons in my classroom. Unlike the Monarch, who splits its skin open to reveal the emerald-like chrysalis inside, the Swallowtail creates a string and it looks like a hammock resting under a stick on an angle. Both caterpillars shed their outer caterpillar body including the legs. Instead of becoming an adult and migrating to Mexico, the Swallowtail will winter over in this sleepy state.

When our caterpillar was no more, I put its chrysalis into a dark cupboard to remain this way until spring. It should have gone into a cool environment imitating natural winter conditions, but I was new at having a Swallowtail and was unaware of that fact.

It wasn't until the last day of school for the kids, that I found it, as I cleaned out a cupboard ready to move to my new classroom. I felt sad and mad at myself, as I had forgotten about it and figured it had died. It looked dry and should have eclosed earlier in the spring. I was going to just throw it out but something told me to put it in the plant pot by the windowsill.

That day at lunch, my students came running down to the staff room bursting with excitement. They claimed that a butterfly was fluttering around our classroom… and sure enough… they were right! A beautiful Swallowtail had awoken in the light and warmth of the early summer sun! I didn't think it was possible, but again I wasn't really surprised. The butterfly adorned the colours of our school; blue and yellow.

We were going to release it as a class, as we said goodbye to a fabulous year and all our friends for the summer, but with the busyness of the last day of school, it just didn't happen.

After school, I returned it to its rightful owner, our principal's husband Bill, so he could have the pleasure of releasing it.

The next day was the staff's last day. Janet had been called to come and see her aging mother as she was nearing the end of her life. She gathered up her things to spend the night at the nursing home, as Bill reminded her that the Swallowtail needed to be released. It was beating its wings wildly, begging for its freedom at that moment.

They went out into the garden and watched as it flew to a nearby tree. It looked down upon them for a while and then flew off into the distance. A few moments later, Janet arrived at her mother's side only to find that she had just missed her passing. That butterfly had been released at the time her mother's spirit was transitioning to the life beyond this earth.

I believe that Swallowtail was meant to be found by Bill. He was guided to be in the right place at the right time, and so was that butterfly.

In the days that followed, Janet continued to see butterflies as she grieved the loss of her dear Mom. A beautiful handmade butterfly quilt had been gently placed on her Mom as they honoured her passing. She was wrapped in the symbol that reminds us of the transition that comes with death and a sense of comfort was created.

Losing a loved one is never easy, but acceptance is easier when we believe that they are in a better place and have given up the confines of an aging body. Whenever Janet sees a butterfly, it quietly reminds her of the many treasured memories she has of her dear Mom.

When Janet speaks of losing her brother in his fifties, shortly after her Mom's death, she tells how even though it was winter, the butterfly symbol kept emerging and giving her comfort. A new little kitten found its way into her life miraculously, as she grieved her loss and she appropriately called her Milkweed. Milkweed is the only food a Monarch caterpillar will eat and therefore very important to the Monarch's survival.

May 11, 2018

Today, Milkweed's Vet clinic posted her photo on Facebook. When her paws are together, they look like…you guessed it! A butterfly!

Photo Credit: Leesa Gillies

Butterfly Gifts

February 8, 2017

One day long ago, when I was all grown up (or so I thought), I came across a candle that I just had to get for my parents. As it burned, it would one day reveal a little crystal butterfly. It came with a small card thanking them for loving me, while allowing me to face my own struggles so I could discover my own life lessons. For it is the struggles that make us strong and prepare us for our journey into the future. When a butterfly struggles to release itself from the chrysalis, it makes its wings stronger and more beautiful in the process. If assisted, its wings can become damaged and it never flies!

A Monarch butterfly eclosing from its chrysalis.

Chantelle's Butterfly

February 8, 2017

I was saddened to learn that one of our grade 6 students had a brain aneurysm and they were unsure what the prognosis would be. Beautiful, blonde Chantelle fought hard and won, as her faith grew stronger. She still had unfinished work here on Earth.

She is now in her twenties, and whenever I see her she has a smile on her face and she just glows with positivity. One day Chantelle was walking down the street. When I spotted her, I pulled over to have a chat. She was excited that she was getting a butterfly tattoo the next day.

I couldn't help but ask if she would share the significance of the butterfly for her. She smiled as she reflected back to the moments just before her brain surgery. Not sure if she was going to make it through, she told her Dad she would come back as a butterfly. She said, "Then I can fly down from heaven and kiss you on the cheek. You will then know I have arrived safely in heaven." It had been a special moment between just the two of them!

Luckily, it was Monarch rearing time and we had a couple of Monarchs that had eclosed that morning. I asked her if she wanted to release them, as their wings would now be dry and they would be ready to go. It would be a celebration of her new tattoo and the beautiful woman she had been given the chance to become.

I always look forward to my chats with Chantelle. She brightens up those lives that are lucky enough to know her and even those who don't.

One day we met and decided to chat at a coffee shop. Neither of us drink coffee, but that day I tried a pumpkin latte. Little did I know that it was laced with espresso coffee. That night I saw 4:00 a.m. before I fell asleep and we still laugh about it.

While we were sitting there, an extremely thin woman sat at the table next to us. We offered to buy her some food but she politely declined. She told us she was waiting for a hospital bed to help her with her eating disorder. Chantelle offered to say a little poem, that she had memorized from a card she had received so long ago, when she was in the hospital fighting for her life. The woman smiled and received the inspirational message she needed that day.

May 15, 2018

Chantelle has always been my cheerleader when it comes to the writing of this book. That day in the coffee shop, she made me write a note to myself on a table napkin, reminding me of my goal to write a book. She always asks, "Is your book done?" or "When can I read it?" She also surprised me with a gift that I treasure...a glass butterfly that hangs in my kitchen window saying, "Believe! All things are possible!" When I was having difficulty believing how this book was coming into being and the synchronicities taking place, it was a much needed reminder to just trust the process. I will always be grateful to Chantelle for her support during this unbelievable time.

I was on my way to a meeting tonight and who did I see out walking her dog?...Chantelle, of course! It was nice to tell her, the writing of the book was complete and publishing would be next. She told me, she was getting another butterfly tattoo.

July, 2018

I was having lunch in the park today, with my good friend, Christi. Who should we see?...but Chantelle. While chatting, Chantelle revealed that her second butterfly tattoo also had a great significance for her and it wasn't related to her illness. It was in memory of her cousin, who had passed away unexpectedly at the age of 16. When they first heard the sad news, they couldn't believe their eyes, as a butterfly fluttered around inside their car... it was January! A cold, snowy Canadian winter day!

The Butterfly's Promise

February 9, 2017

I remember driving through the worst snowstorm ever! There was no turning back, for the funeral of our 17-year-old nephew was that day. A dark and dreary day it was! Losing someone so young is never easy, especially when they had a promising future ahead of them. It was heart wrenching to see his young friends comfort each other as they tried to make sense of their loss.

In the weeks that lay ahead, I found words circulating in my brain until I knew I had to write them down. They were hauntingly persistent. It was so foreign to me and I couldn't explain what was happening. There was just this knowing, like I had never experienced before. Piece by piece the following poem materialized in the year 2000.

Over the years, this poem has travelled to many funerals, including that of my parents. My daughter had it put on notecards, and being a nurse, gives one to families mourning the loss of their loved ones. Its message is timeless and comforting. Through the years, the poem has resurfaced as the need has arisen.

The Butterfly's Promise

When you left your earthly home the butterflies began to dance
And sing a little song of hope that there's a second chance
To live some place much better where there's no hurt or pain.
The earth's great loss we feel today turns into heaven's gain.
The memories we'll always treasure and you'll live within our hearts.
Forever we will love you...Saying good-bye's the hardest part.
We'll miss your loving smile, your jokes, your laugh, your love.
We know you'll look down from heaven and guide us from above.
Until we meet again when we leave our earthly home.
The journey will not be feared knowing we won't be alone.
Each time we see a butterfly floating through the air.
We'll hear it's whispered promise that you're waiting for us up there.
For death is nothing more than the time to spread our wings.
We'll soar above this earth towards bigger and better things.

Written by Barb Hacking

Rainbows

February 9, 2017

My good friend, Sue was nearing the end of her chemotherapy treatments, for breast cancer, when her son's fiancé died unexpectedly from a brain aneurysm at the age of 22. There was no warning, no goodbyes and she was gone.

It was September and prime time for Monarchs to be migrating. One of ours had eclosed the day before the funeral and my husband and I drove to Point Pelee National Park. This is where many of the Monarchs gather before crossing Lake Erie into the United States, as they begin their long journey to Mexico. We released a butterfly for Renée at the most southern tip of Canada. It was reluctant at first and then it flew to my heart. When it was ready, the butterfly flew upwards and I couldn't help but think you could see her flying towards a cloud that look like an angel with its hands out to receive her.

On the day of Renée's Celebration of Life, it was very dreary and the rain cried from the dark clouds above. I remember praying that there would be a rainbow for this grieving family and their friends, but that was not to be. The rain continued.

I offered the family some Monarchs to release in Renée's memory the day after the funeral. In contrast to the day before, the sun shone down on this peaceful Sunday morning. Miraculously, I had enough butterflies for each family member to have one of their own.

When Renée's father released his butterfly, it flew to his shoulder and just stayed there for the longest time. He walked around the garden and when the time was right it flew towards the heavens.

Renée's mom released hers and a few minutes later she found a Monarch sitting quietly on the deck. She reached out for it with her hand and the butterfly crawled onto it. It walked up her arm to her face as if to place a kiss upon her cheek, and finally it too joined the others.

I saw smiles that morning on people who I thought would never smile again. Renée would have wanted that!

When all of the butterflies had been released, a rainbow appeared directly over the garden. Interestingly enough, there was no rain… just a blue sunny sky and a rainbow perfectly arched over the garden.

Renée's mother says that now when she sees a butterfly, it makes her heart sparkle.

One year later, Sue released a Monarch in memory of Renée. She will never be forgotten but cancer will be, as she released a butterfly symbolizing her return to good health once again.

June 26, 2018

When reviewing the story with Sue, she had butterfly stories of her own to share with me. Being open to these special visits allows us to receive the heartfelt messages that they bring.

May 30, 2018

I saw this rainbow phenomenon once before. My dear childhood friend, Caroline and her husband Garry, had lost their precious 15 year old son Nathan, due to cancer. Caroline, who now lives in Scotland, was visiting and we decided to do a Monarch release at Webster's Falls in Dundas, Ontario to celebrate Nathan's life. It was a lovely autumn day but we discovered that it was too chilly for the Monarch to fly. The release would have to wait! This Monarch needed to get on its way to Mexico before the colder weather set in, but first it needed to spend more time with Caroline.

Driving home we saw the most beautiful double rainbow...and there was no rain.

The evening of the butterfly release for Renee, I got a phone call from my friend Christine, who had graciously helped me typeset the poem, "The Butterfly's Promise" with one of our photographs for Renée's family. She said, "Barb, there was a reason you asked me to help you with your poem." She then asked if she could give the poem to her friends who had just lost their 17-year-old son, Scott. She also wondered, if by chance, I had one more butterfly for the parents to release at his grave. Of course I did; the last one of the season!

A Tribute to Celebrate Scott's Life

April 30, 2018

This morning I received an email that really touched my heart, from Scott's Mother, Sherri. I had just placed the previous paragraph into the manuscript.

"Good Morning Barb,

This message is so embarrassingly overdue.....Barb, there are no words to thank you for your kindness....truly there aren't. Some friends of ours - Ken and Christine, gave us the butterfly from you, to release the day of my son Scott's, funeral - and also, more recently than that, gave me your butterfly book - in honor of Scott - who tragically left this world, September 18, 2015 - something I will never ever recover from, not until I get to Heaven and can hold him again.

We released the beautiful butterfly at the graveside service for Scott, and it hovered and circled around us for some time, before it flew away - it was INCREDIBLE!! A moment that is forever etched in our hearts and minds. Butterflies have since been our sign/symbol that Scott is always near us. I read your book frequently, and actually, I can recite it from cover to cover! It is sitting on the coffee table in my living room - it always brings me such great comfort. Thank you for your kind words written inside the front cover of the book.

Again, words cannot even begin to convey how your kindness warmed not only my heart, but also everyone else who has been on this grief journey with us. Everyone who was at the gravesite, when we said our final goodbyes to our precious Scott - still comment to this day, on the butterfly and what meaning it brought to our farewell to him. To think that a complete stranger, as you were, could have touched us so profoundly by your kindness and thoughtfulness. As I've said, the words to thank you, are completely inadequate!! You truly have no idea how your love shone through, and still does to this day, at such a tragic time in our lives.

You truly have no idea how meaningful the butterfly release was the day of the funeral.... Honestly-it is talked about so often, and left us with such a tender memory in the most tragic time in our lives.

As broken and shattered as our hearts were and still are, having Scott "go home" ahead of us, your butterfly gave us hope.

God Bless you Barb, Sherri"

"Dear Sherri,

Thank you so much for your heartfelt email! It was perfectly timed. I am writing a book about how butterflies speak to us in so many ways and about so many things, including death. I believe that you were meant to have that butterfly and I was just guided to give it to you with Christine's help. It was our last Monarch that year! I had done a butterfly release the day before Christine contacted me, to see if by chance, I had one more precious butterfly. It was meant for you. It's a miracle, and what I call Monarch magic. Christine helped me prepare the "Butterfly's Promise" to give to the grieving family of another young person just days before you lost your precious son. It had been written long ago when we lost our 17 year old nephew. Again, I felt that the poem was a gift through me, not by me, to those experiencing a huge loss of a loved one. It has resurfaced many times over the years. I hope to publish it so it is available for anyone who needs its message. I know it found its way to you by the grace of our Creator.

You don't know how much your email has meant to me and how the timing was impeccable. I was up until 2:00 a.m. editing my book, "When a Butterfly Speaks... Whispered Life Lessons". I awoke this morning with the lovely sunshine streaming in through the window and was greeted with your very special email. You certainly got my day off to a wonderful start!

Last summer I had lots of Monarchs after many years of not seeing many at all. If this year we are lucky to have some more, I would love to meet you and do a butterfly release for Scott, if that is something you would like to do. Again, you can let me know your wishes. I believe we have been connected for a reason. There are no coincidences! Thank you again for sharing your very personal experience with me.

Sending you bear hugs and butterfly kisses!"

Barb Hacking

"A miracle is never lost. It may touch many people you have not even met, and produce undreamed of changes in situations of which you are not even aware." (Text 1.45.1-2. The Course of Miracles)

June 29, 2018

Sherri, her Mother and I, met today on a perfect summer afternoon, to release a Monarch in memory of Scott. I was greeted by the most beautiful smile when Sherri came to my car. What an honour and privilege it was to witness the love they had for this amazing young man. I was surprised to learn that Scott was raising caterpillars at the time of his death.

Sherri's whispered message for her precious son accompanied the butterfly. It lingered for quite some time. In fact, we were able to retrieve it for a second release. Each time, the Monarch was facing

Sherri, as it lifted into the air. There were white billowy clouds in only one part of the sky, and that's where the Monarch eventually went. When it was ready, it just lifted gracefully and was off!

Finding the Calm After the Storm
(Material Possessions) or (Forgiveness)

February 15, 2017

Butterflies flying amongst the fragrant garden flowers have always made me feel happy inside. Their exquisite colours dancing through life, make me delight in the simple things. They are for everyone. Rich or poor, young or old, male or female, if only they choose to pause for a moment and catch that glorious calm that watching graceful butterflies can bring. This valuable lesson that they have taught, has helped me time and time again.

A short time ago, I discovered that my wedding rings had been stolen from my jewellery box along with other valuables, including my gold butterfly ring my staff had given me when I retired. During the time that followed, I felt sad and heartbroken...even angry. There had been no break in, so it had to be someone I knew which made it even more difficult to accept. No money could ever replace the sentimental value that those rings held for me. Rings from our engagement, our wedding day, our first and tenth anniversaries among others. I remained hopeful that they would be returned. As the days passed, I faced the realization that I was probably not going to see them again. The storm that brewed within me needed to die down and I needed to find the calm that I treasured once again. I felt like there was a busy bee buzzing around my brain, not the calm of a gentle graceful butterfly. Every second was consumed thinking about my rings. I felt betrayed and I grieved their loss.

I came to realize that these material objects, however beautiful, did not hold the special memories I had attached to them. I still had those and nobody could take them away. Deep within, I knew that the love that brought those rings to my finger, still remained; and love is the greatest gift of all! We all have it in us to give. The best things in life are the simple things. No money needed, and they are such a treasure!

March 11, 2017

After writing this story, I thought I had put the situation to rest by depositing my emotions on the paper, but that was not the case. About a week later, I was surprised at the anger that boiled inside of me. Not an emotion I was proud of or enjoyed, but needed to feel. It is one of the stages of grieving that would have sat there until I decided to let it surface. It wasn't until I totally forgave the person who took my rings, that I achieved the inner peace I was looking for. There just happened to be a meditation about forgiveness on Facebook that day and it was the answer I was looking for. It helped me return to the person I was, before this temporary life distraction took place.

March 21, 2018

Today I came across a scrapbook I had created for the Monarch Teacher Network. It was my ticket to travel with other Canadian and American teachers to the overwintering grounds of the Monarch butterfly back in 2005. It contained a poem I had written for a school assembly we had, as we entered the new millennium. It demonstrates that forgiveness is the key to achieving peace within ourselves and with those around us. Forgiving isn't always easy, but it's necessary to achieve peace.

The Peaceful Butterfly
(Written November, 1999)

February 11, 2017

Butterfly, you fly so high,
Over the rainbow, up in the sky.
If only we could learn from you,
How to be peaceful and loving too!

Butterfly, you are small, yet strong,
Please teach the world to get along.
Maybe we can learn from you,
How to be peaceful and loving too!

You live your life with beauty and grace,
You bring a smile to a frowning face.
Perhaps we can learn from you.
How to be peaceful and loving too!

Butterfly, you don't make a sound,
Yet, you're able to spread joy around.
As we watch, we learn from you,
How to be peaceful and loving too!

You grow and change with so much ease,
Teach us your secret,
Oh wouldn't you please. Then we might learn from you,
How to be peaceful and loving too!

Butterfly, you forgive and forget.
It's the lesson we haven't mastered yet.
Because when we do, we'll have learned from you,
How to be peaceful and loving too!

Each student wrote their wish of peace for the new millennium on a paper butterfly. The butterflies were arranged into a colourful rainbow on the gym wall symbolizing the beauty created when we all work together towards a common goal of peace. "The Peaceful Butterfly" was written as we prepared to begin an exciting new millennium. We were so full of hope and dreams, which really can become a reality, if each of us does our part. We could learn from the mistakes mankind has made in the past. We wanted to enter the new millennium with a song of peace in our hearts and create a world where we live in harmony with those around us. We have so much to learn from the butterfly who lives such a peaceful existence. It is no wonder that these delicate, whimsical creatures add such beauty to our earth and are a symbol of peace, hope and transformation.

Death of a Furry Friend

February 15, 2017

Our black, huggable, furry kitty named Bear (that's the name the Humane Society had given him. Odd name for a cat!) left us almost as quickly as he came into our lives. One morning, Bear was found at the side of our house sick and weak. We rushed him to the vet's, but there was nothing they could do.

When we returned home heartbroken, we discovered that four of our caterpillars had transformed into chrysalids while we were gone. We decided as a family, that we would mourn until they became butterflies. Then we would release them in memory of our dear Bear and rejoice that he had been a part of our lives, even for a short time.

There is an old native legend that "If you whisper a message to a butterfly, it will take it to a loved one in the heavens". So that's what we did!

Butterfly Buddies

February 15, 2017

I am grateful to have met so many wonderful people who also share my passion for Monarch butterflies. I have appreciated them sharing their experiences and knowledge.

When I first started inviting Monarchs into my classroom, I was lucky to have my biologist husband showing me the ropes. He grew up surrounded by nature and spent his childhood days exploring everything from snakes to rocks. It's no wonder he became an enthusiastic biology teacher.

We were celebrating our first anniversary at the glorious bed and breakfast on Blue Mountain, where we had spent the last night of our honeymoon, just outside of Collingwood, Ontario. We met a young English couple while hiking the trails there and discovered a Monarch caterpillar munching on its milkweed lunch. (Milkweed is the only food the larva will eat.) They were so fascinated by the Monarch's story and intently listened to Mark as he shared his vast knowledge with them. We decided to take the caterpillar back to Stratford for my classroom. We also brought the English couple with us. As we drove back home the caterpillar magically became a chrysalis and our new-found friends were even more intrigued. Their excitement was contagious!

Shortly thereafter, school began and my teaching days with the Monarchs were launched. My students curiously watched the chrysalis as it became transparent, revealing the magnificent creature within. Right before their eyes, the butterfly pushed itself out of its home that it had hidden in for the past 14 days. Upside down like a trapeze artist, it clung to the empty chrysalis shell. It's abdomen swollen like a balloon began to pump fluid into the tiny wings. The wings expanded until you couldn't help but wonder how something so large could have ever fit into the tiny enclosure in the first place.

Teaching the children to respect nature includes releasing the butterfly as soon as it was ready. After several hours the wings were dry and it began to move around the enclosure. In nature, the butterfly usually ecloses in the morning ready to dry its wings in the sunshine. If it is a rainy or cloudy day, it seems that the butterfly within, senses that it probably should wait to eclose under more suitable weather conditions.

There is nothing like watching the children's excitement and delight as their friend flies upward and onward, enjoying its new found freedom. This would become my most treasured teaching moment over and over again, in the years to come. It's an experience that never grows old and remains just as exciting to this very day, especially as the population has declined, when compared to days gone by!

Even though I am retired, I just love sharing this experience with others, ready to be touched by Monarch magic.

It wasn't until 2003, that I had heard of the Monarch Teachers' Network where I discovered others, both in Canada and the United States, who were just as passionate as I was about the Monarch Butterfly. I was so disappointed to find that their summer workshop was full. I quickly got my name on the list for the following summer. My teaching colleague, Kate, and I were gifted with three wonderful days of being with like-minded souls learning even more! Erik Mollenhauer, our workshop master from New Jersey, was eager to transfer his immense knowledge to the lucky teachers who had the pleasure of learning with the Monarchs. To this day, I continue to discover new found secrets of this amazing insect and have had the privilege of volunteering at Monarch Teacher workshops over the years. Kate continues to enrich her children's and students' lives with Monarch magic.

In February 2005, just weeks after my dear father's passing, I was honored to travel to Mexico with a fellowship provided by the Monarch Teachers' Network, where I connected with Canadian and American teachers. While there, we were able to visit with Mexican teachers and their students. We traveled to Cerro Pelon and El Rosario Monarch Sanctuaries where the lush Oyamel fir trees grow on the mountains. It is here that the Monarchs east of the Rocky mountains travel to each winter. (The ones west of the Rockies travel to Southern California and the Baja peninsula .) They cling to the trees during cooler weather, the tree trunks acting as a hot water bottle for their bellies. When the sun warms their surroundings, they fly like a snowstorm of butterflies, dancing and nectaring, on the nearby flowers and sipping water from nearby puddles. This was a life-changing experience. I knew when I returned home I would never be the same again. As the population began to decline, I knew I would join many others who were inspired to protect them. I was more dedicated than ever to help preserve this incredible insect and also learned the importance of creating butterfly gardens, at schools to help teach our young people.

Social media began to create a network for those with a similar interest. It is so easy now to keep in touch, share experiences, follow the migration and entice newbies to the clan. I enjoy seeing what's happening on the Mexican mountains, thousands of kilometres away, through Facebook videos, photos and posts. People can take a trip to the mountains without ever leaving their home. They can meet and learn from others without ever coming face-to-face. Technology is indeed amazing!

Be sure to check out the following Facebook pages!

When a Butterfly Speaks...Whispered Life Lessons
Monarchs Migrating through Ontario
The Beautiful Monarch
Monarch Teacher Network
Ontario Gardeners
Journey North
Monarch Watch

My Retirement Dream
Comes True (Finally!)

February 22, 2017

It is this technology that brought me to Darlene Burgess. She is an avid Monarch lover, raiser, tagger, observer and protector who has a Monarch Waystation not too far from Point Pelee National Park. She is the official Monarch monitor at the park during the fall migration.

In September, 2015, Mark and I were wishing to pay the park a visit. It had always been a dream of mine to go there, the September I retired. It was however, not to be, as there were too few Monarchs that year.

Being a three hour drive each way, we wanted to make sure that the conditions for seeing Monarchs were just perfect. Darlene had been posting on Facebook, that there were indeed Monarchs to be seen. (A rarity for the past few years.)

All we were seeing in Stratford was rain, and Monarchs simply do not fly in the rain. Darlene assured us that there were plenty of Monarchs and the sun was shining in great profusion in the park. We decided to take the chance, and after driving through a torrential downpour all the way to the other side of London, an hour away, we were greeted with glorious sunshine and one of our best Monarch experiences ever.

Many Monarch butterflies were nectaring in the goldenrod patches, creating fat reserves for their 2300 mile trek to the mountains in Mexico. (3,856 km from Point Pelee.) They would roost high up in the trees for the night and when the weather and wind conditions were perfect, they would fly across the Great Lake and be on their winter-escaping journey southward.

We were in our glory photographing butterflies of all kinds that were basking in the warm sunshine. Chatting with others who shared these precious moments with us, was another highlight. Mark and I then walked the forested path that led to the most southern tip of Canada.

Ahead of me, Mark was being followed by a Monarch. When he stopped to take a picture, the butterfly stopped too. Mesmerized, I quickly caught up and noticed the butterfly resting on a branch. It allowed me to very gently pick it up and I discovered it had a tag on it, from Monarch Watch. This is an organization in the United States that helps track the amazing migration of these traveling friends. The number on the tag coincides with information registered with Monarch Watch, such as who tagged it, and where and when the butterfly was released.

We photographed the tag before reaching the water at the end of the path, where we happily released it.

Moments later, who would we meet, but Darlene Burgess for the first time, in person. We discovered that the tagged butterfly was one she had released three days earlier, at her farm. We kid Darlene that we met her butterfly, before we met her.

The rest of the evening was spent looking for Monarch roosts in the trees before the sun set on this awesome, eventful day. Several were found, with much excitement, before heading back home, with many treasured memories.

This was my retirement dream come true. I just had to wait a few years. I'm sure that made me appreciate it all the more, as I've always believed that good things are worth waiting for!

Point Pelee is such a magical place! It's no wonder the Monarchs gather here!

Wedding Wishes

Jennifer's Wedding

February 15, 2017

Trying to time having Monarchs to release, for a celebration of any kind, whether it be a celebration of life, or a wedding, is practically impossible with the decline of the Monarchs. By fluke, we discovered one lonely caterpillar. We were hoping it would eclose on our niece's wedding day. We left for the wedding disappointed, as it was still in its chrysalis. The wedding was held in the downtown of a busy city, so it probably wasn't the best spot to release it anyway.

Returning from the wedding late that night, we discovered a beautiful butterfly hanging peacefully at the top of the enclosure. with its wings fully dry. It had come out on the day of Jennifer's wedding to Kevin!

A family get together was being held the next day, for the bride and groom, so they happily released their butterfly in a lovely garden. It flew to a nearby tree, watched over the festivities for a while and then gracefully fluttered away, leaving the newlyweds to enjoy their new life, as man and wife.

Rachel's Wedding

Our daughter Rachel, and her husband Jeff, got married on a gorgeous day in August, 2015 in Niagara Falls. Releasing Monarchs was a possibility, but was becoming complicated with the busyness of wedding preparations, the scarcity of caterpillars and the logistics and safety of trying to transport them to the out-of-town wedding. It was decided to have Lisa Jensen release her snowy-white peace doves instead, and that turned out to be an absolutely beautiful addition to the celebration.

We were delighted to see so many white Cabbage butterflies dancing around the fragrant garden where the reception was being held, in Niagara-on-the-Lake. They looked as though they had flown off of Rachel and Jeff's cake, which was adorned with delicate white butterflies, created with icing. Having live ones in the garden was a bonus.

Surprisingly, one Monarch came along for a wee visit as the guests relaxed in the garden, posed for a photo, wished the newlyweds the best and then flew off into the distance. We didn't have to do a thing. It just showed up at the right time and made the wedding day complete. Monarch magic!

That Thanksgiving, Mark and I returned to the Niagara area and rented a pair of eco-scooters to celebrate his birthday. We had so much fun exploring the exquisite Niagara Parkway, as the weather was divine.

We stopped to talk to another couple and noticed a Monarch flying past us. We were surprised to see one so late in the season, as most of its Monarch friends would be well on their way to Mexico. All of a sudden, the Monarch darted out on to the road and was hit by an SUV. My heart plummeted from sheer joy to sadness as I asked Mark to retrieve its lifeless body. I couldn't bear to let it get run over.

I just happened to have an empty candy tin in my purse, so I placed the Monarch carefully in it and closed the lid. I put the tin back in my purse and we continued on our way, feeling very forlorn. We were led to a meadow filled with sweet scented wildflowers. Mark and I stopped to lay the butterfly to rest but when we opened the box, it moved. It crawled on to my finger, paused as if to say thank you, and flew to a nearby tree. Time stood still as we waited to see if it was strong enough to fly a greater distance. It posed for a few more photos, and then it spread its wings and was off on its migratory journey. Another Monarch magic moment to add to our list!

Losing a Student

February 23, 2017

It was Remembrance Day. Mark and I walked to a nearby cemetery to pay our respects to the people who had given their lives for our freedom. It was late in the season so we were very surprised to see little white butterflies, not only at the war graves but at the gravesites of former students.

One of the most heartbreaking events in a teacher's life is losing a student. The death of someone so young, is hard to accept.

I can remember releasing many Monarch butterflies as a school, honouring the wonderful student we had lost. It was in the days where there were lots of Monarchs around, preparing to migrate to Mexico and being raised in our classrooms.

Again, releasing butterflies is a beautiful tribute to someone who is so dear to our hearts, and allows us to exhibit gratitude for being lucky enough to have known them.

When I see butterflies dancing gracefully upwards, I can't help but think of the beautiful human spirit that still exists, but in a different form. All the feelings I have, when releasing butterflies were eventually transferred to the words in the poem, "The Butterfly's Promise".

March 29, 2018

This past summer was an amazing year for raising Monarch butterflies. This is something we hadn't seen for quite some time. It gave me the opportunity to take a Monarch for each student I had lost and release it in their memory. These students are gone, but not forgotten.

Traveling to Mexico

February 23, 2017

Traveling to Mexico in February, 2005, with fellow Canadian and American teachers was definitely one of the highlights of my life. Although I have loved butterflies for as long as I can remember, that experience was truly life-changing. It was there, sitting on the mountain surrounded by these magnificent creatures that I couldn't help but feel in awe of the beauty and messages they bring to our world. The sound of their fluttering wings was music to my ears. I never wanted to lose the feeling I had at that very moment. It is so etched in my memory that I can return to that place, mentally, when I need peace or calm in my life… and I often do.

I had just lost my wonderful father, but I knew he was now free to fly, and had escaped the confines of an aging body. He was an active man for 90 years. During the last five months of his life, his body was like a chrysalis restricting his movement and freedom. These butterflies dancing all around my grieving soul, reminded me that although I missed him immensely, he was now free to fly.

When I returned from Mexico, I promised Mark that someday I would return to these magnificent Monarch-filled mountains with him, by my side. I knew he would love it!

Mark and I had started dating in 1976. That was the year National Geographic announced to the world that the mystery of where the Monarchs go in the winter, was solved. Scientists had discovered the secret that some of the local people had known forever. So 40 years to the day since our first date, Mark and I were climbing the Mexican Sierra Madre mountains. It seemed the perfect place to celebrate our 40 years of Monarch memories. When climbing a mountain belonging to the Monarchs, I call it the stairway to heaven, which happened to be the song of our first dance. We had nothing but sunshine and blue skies. We couldn't have chosen a better place.

Yes, the trees behind us are covered
in Monarch Butterflies!

Dia de los Muertos
(Day of the Dead)

February 23, 2017

At the beginning of November, the Mexican people see lots of Monarchs coming to their mountains to escape the cold winter. For many years the Mexican people have believed that these butterflies are the spirits of their dead ancestors, returning to them for a visit. They leave out food, sweets and other tributes for them, and it is a time of great celebration for all to enjoy! This day is known as Dia de los Muertos, in Spanish.

Where do the Monarchs go in the winter?

All the Monarchs that enjoy the meadows of Canada and United States east of the Rockies settle on the Sierra Madre mountains, nestled in Central Mexico. They roost on the Oyamel fir trees at the top of the mountains, snuggling together to keep warm during the cooler temperatures, especially at night. When the sun warms their tiny bodies, they fly freely, never bumping into each other. It truly is an amazing sight!

Monarchs west of the Rockies migrate to the warmer climate in southern California. This is a much shorter migration of 500 miles and the Monarchs roost on Eucalyptus trees. This is on our bucket list for the near future.

Back to the Magical
Monarch Mountains

February 23, 2017

Before Christmas, I discovered this longing I had, to return to the mountains once again. Mark thought perhaps in five years he would like to go back. I laid the idea to rest for the time being, but in early January I heard of Sara Dykman and her Butterbike Project. She was planning to follow the Monarch migration, beginning in Mexico at the Monarch mountains, and then follow them up through the United States and into Canada. Then she planned to follow the migration back to Mexico, once again. All on her bike! No, not a motorized one!

Interestingly, the Monarchs that make it to Mexico are not the same butterflies that will return to the Northern United States and Canada. The generation in Mexico will mate in the spring, the males will die, and the females will carry the eggs to Texas and beyond, and then they too will die. It's their offspring that will continue the migration northward. In fact they say, it's their great grandchildren that come to Canada.

Sarah posted several of her proposed routes on Facebook. I was so disappointed that none of them included Southern Ontario. There were so many Monarch lovers here that she just had to meet, and she couldn't miss Point Pelee, the Monarch's favorite migration spot, connecting the Canadian and American migration. I sent her a message and coincidentally, so did Darlene Burgess who lives near Point Pelee National Park.

I was ecstatic when Sara messaged me back saying she was considering a route change, and even more so when she said she'd be coming to Stratford, in August and would include Point Pelee, as well.

It was then that I knew I needed to go back to the mountains. Within an hour, I had a room and flight to Mexico booked. It was meant to be!

Sara would be able to join me for the week exploring Monarch sanctuaries and then I would be there to see her off on this awesome adventure of hers. Darlene Burgess, from Point Pelee would also be there to see her off! Coincidence? Miracle? Synchronicity? Magic?

Tomorrow, I am off to Mexico and I will leave this part of the writing until I return. I know that the week will be filled with many magical moments...

Facing Fears

March 4, 2017

And it was!

Just after I had booked my trip, I begin to hear of events in Mexico that made me wonder if I had made the right decision, to travel alone. Many people expressed their concern for my safety. I decided that if fear got in my way, I wouldn't put to rest this burning desire to return to the Monarch mountains once again. My love for the Monarchs trumped all fears. If Sarah Dykman could travel on a bike alone, I surely was able to travel by car, bus and plane.

Taking a taxi from the airport to the bus station, in Mexico City, amidst a mountain of traffic, I happened to see a Swallowtail and another bright yellow butterfly playing tag outside the window. They reminded me to breathe and just enjoy the sunshine and the anticipation of the adventures that lay ahead. Even among the chaos of the crowded, bustling city they peacefully meandered along their way. I could follow their fine example too.

Heaven Here on Earth

February 24, 2017

My goal was to get to JM Butterfly Bed and Breakfast before dark. Mark and I had stayed there the year before and were treated royally by Joel and Ellen, the owners and their family. It is the perfect spot to stay if you want to see the Monarch sanctuaries and get a taste of their heaven here on earth. Delicious authentic Mexican food awaits you right next door cooked by Joel's Mother, Rosa, and her daughters. Need I say more?

Be sure to check out their website to find out more about their mission. Butterflies and their People was created to educate others and help the Monarchs.(http.//jmbutterflybnb.com/our-mission/)

I was treated to the most beautiful sunset as the taxi drove up the mountain to Macheros. It was breathtaking! The orange hues of the sunset reminded me of my beloved Monarchs as I neared their home. I arrived just as the fiery ball was burying its head below the mountain tops. It looked like Mother Nature had water-coloured the sky. I felt like I had died and gone to heaven.

Take Time to Smell the Roses Or
When a Butterfly Speaks...Listen!

February 25, 2017

Sara Dykman had arrived shortly before me and we hugged hello. Seeing each other face to face for the first time, I felt like I had known her forever. That's the way it is with us crazy Monarch maniacs. We conversed over a delicious Mexican meal and then went off to bed exhausted. Sara had ridden up the mountain to Macheros on her well-equipped bike and I had been up since 2:00 a.m.

It was great waking up with the bright Mexican sunshine streaming in the window providing a break from the snowy days back home. Walking to breakfast I saw my first Monarch. The tropical milkweed along the path was laden with caterpillars and eggs. Macheros has a local population of Monarchs that stay year-round.

The little boy who lives right beside the bed and breakfast, Jesus, was anxious to show us his caterpillars. He was no more than two years old and already knew to respect and not touch his friends living just outside the door of his home. We enjoyed interacting! Him in Spanish, me in English and of course Sarah, in both languages.

Recuperating from traveling the day before, we decided to hike up the smaller mountain behind our bed and breakfast to get us into shape for the trek up the Monarch mountain, Cerro Pelon, the next day. As you walk up, you can feel your breath being taxed due to the change in altitude. If you pause for a few seconds, your body acclimatizes and you are ready to go on until you feel winded again.

The challenging climb was sure worth it as we entered the meadow at the top. It was filled with fragrant, vividly-coloured wildflowers, butterflies and bees dancing, and birds singing. My white, winter skin welcomed the sun. Heaven simply can't get any better than this! So untouched by man!

As I sat there writing, an orange butterfly landed right beside me. It wasn't a Monarch. They were all on top of the mountain beside this one. She allowed me to video and photograph her. Then she beckoned me to follow her and let her show me how beautiful her meadow was. So I did!

I'm sure she was telling me to set my writing aside for the moment. How often do we not really enjoy the experience as we multitask, or hide behind a camera or get lost in our cell phone? Even though she didn't make a sound, I clearly got the message.

A hummingbird motored past my ear. It hovered at one flower and then moved to another. There were so many sensory pleasures awaiting my discovery. Two, snow white Sulphur butterflies chased each other. Bees were buzzing and enjoying the sweet nectar from flowers of every color. The music was provided by the sweet sounding, cheerful birds.

Mark and I had visited this meadow the year before and I often return anytime my heart desires, as the memories are etched vividly in the photo album in my mind. It is definitely one of my happy places.

The rest of the week was spent visiting the Monarch sanctuaries and talking to like-minded people. At the top of Cerro Pelon, we had a group of Mexican, Canadian and American people interacting in perfect harmony, as the Monarchs fluttered around us and we stood in awe at their beauty. This is the world as it should be, rejoicing in our similarities and accepting our differences.

One of the most magical moments was on the road to Piedra Herrada Butterfly sanctuary with Linh and Erica, from New York City, who had become instant friends. The Monarchs were fluttering out of the forest and flying in masses down the road. I had never seen anything like it as millions of Monarchs flew past us, as we stood on the road. They just streamed like a rapidly moving brook. Most of the traffic moved slowly, however, there were a few speeding trucks that just kept motoring through this kaleidoscope of Monarchs. (Kaleidoscope is the collective name for a group of butterflies.) You would see the Monarchs that couldn't make it out of the way in time, embedded in their grills on their front hood. With schedules to keep, the Monarchs were just in their way. It saddened me to see man and nature collide.

My favourite souvenir of this moment was a slow-motion video which took me back to being surrounded by millions of Monarchs. When placed on Facebook it had over 35,000 views in the first week. Oh, the power of the Internet; allowing people to experience that precious moment too! This video can be seen on my Facebook page. "When a Butterfly Speaks...Whispered Life Lessons"

Some people said the Monarchs were coming down from the mountain to get water and then would return before sunset. Perhaps they had already started their migration. They appeared to know what they were doing, where they were going. and they were all moving in the same direction without ever colliding. It truly was a sight to see! The sound of their flapping wings was mesmerizing as they sped past in their hurry to go who knows where. It felt like a snowstorm of butterflies being pushed forward by the wind. Their shadows moved just as quickly on the pavement below.

And She's Off!
Sara Dykman Begins Her Journey

March 2, 2017

Of course, the highlight of the trip was getting to know Sara Dykman and seeing her off on her incredible Butterbike journey following the Monarch migration. At 11:00 a.m. on Thursday, March 2, Sarah's bike was neatly packed carrying her home and equipment for the next nine months. The Monarchs were starting to leave! Sara now knew where they had been and she was ready to set off too! As Sara was just finishing her packing, there was a single Monarch circling around her which I happened to video tape. I was in awe as I watched it, as Sara prepared to leave. Again, it's presence was so perfectly orchestrated. It finally landed on the hill overlooking Sara's bike and I'm sure it was thanking her for her courage, time and effort, to make people aware of their situation.

Her courage inspired me to travel to Mexico alone. That courage would take her on the adventure of a lifetime, all the while making people aware of the importance of planting milkweed for our Monarch friends, as well as nectar-rich plants. Protecting their habitat while increasing awareness of their declining population is necessary to ensure their survival.

Planting for the Monarchs

March 4, 2017

When I travelled to the Monarch mountains in 2005, with the Monarch Teacher Network, I was lucky enough to connect and travel with American teachers, who were already planting butterfly gardens at their schools. I was so inspired, as they enthusiastically told me how exciting it was for the students to learn about Monarchs and their dependence on the proper habitat. I came back, only to hear that our school campus was moving to an abandoned grade seven and eight school. So four years later, the funding had been collected and the empty school grounds was ready for a transformation. There was nothing but grass, a few trees and asphalt. Hardly a welcoming habitat for a butterfly! Or a child, for that matter!

During the month of June in 2009, every child in the school did their part to create the new Avon School Butterfly Peace Garden. The fundraising was complete. The right people and their tools arrived when needed. Parents who were professional landscapers lent us their expertise and equipment. Co-op students guided the planting each day. The Northwestern Secondary School teenagers and their buddies from Alberta came one day after school and demonstrated that many hands make light work. Forty teenagers dug six gardens in two hours. It was an extremely hot day and they had been dragon boating beforehand, but they didn't complain.

Magically and easily, the gardens were created and ready for the many Monarchs and other pollinators that would enjoy their new home. Avon School's garden became Stratford's first Monarch Waystation recognized and registered by Monarch Watch in the United States. (http:/www.monarchwatch.org) Monarch Waystations are specially designed habitats for Monarchs. They include milkweed plants, which are the only food source for the Monarchs' caterpillars. These patches serve as breeding and nectaring areas for the adult Monarchs.

The flowers of milkweed have the most beautiful smell and are enjoyed by many other pollinators, as well. I often say that we should change the name of milkweed to milkflower. Nectar plants are also included. They provide energy for the adults, especially during their long migration to the overwintering grounds in Mexico.

In order to plant milkweed, which was considered a noxious weed up until 2014 in the province of Ontario, my students made a presentation to Stratford's City Council dressed like Monarchs at various stages of their life cycle. The kids taught our city leaders that without milkweed, the Monarchs would not survive. They ended their presentation by blowing milkweed seeds around the council chambers and were greeted by a standing ovation, and permission to plant milkweed... and we did.

So Stratford. even before the drastic decline of the Monarch butterfly population, recognized the need to help. and even broke a few rules in the process. It wasn't until 2014 that milkweed was taken off the noxious weed list by the Ontario government. I wish I could say this was true for every province and state, lucky enough to be a part of the Monarchs' migratory path. Without milkweed, Monarchs simply will not survive.

It is said that if you plant milkweed, the Monarchs will come, and they did. At least they did up until I retired in June, 2012. I found seven caterpillars as I left the school on my final day of school in June, but that September they were virtually impossible to find. I had dreamed of being able to give Monarch larvae to teachers so that their students could marvel in the miracle of the Monarch, but that was not to be. At least not that year!

I also thought, instead of going back to school in September, I would love to visit Point Pelee National Park and see the Monarchs gathering for their flight across Lake Erie, but that year the park didn't even have enough Monarchs to do an official count. It was frightening!

The annual count of the population in Mexico's overwintering grounds, revealed the lowest number of Monarchs, ever. According to Monarch Watch, there were 18.19 hectares of trees covered in Monarchs in the Mexican biosphere in 1996-1997. This year there were only 1.19 hectares and scientists were very concerned. The following year there were even less; 0.67 hectares. By 2015-2016 the population was on the increase (4.01 hectares) until a devastating ice storm hit the Oyamel Fir forests, where the Monarchs were escaping the Canadian and Northern State's winter. Mark and I were excited to see so many Monarchs when we visited the Mexican sanctuaries in February 2016, and then the ice storm hit, in early March. Snow and ice in Mexico is virtually unheard of. In Canada, we were having early Spring weather. Could this devastating event be due to climate change? There is no way to count how many Monarchs actually perished due to this natural disaster, but it was estimated that 30-50% were lost depending on who you talk to.

With the bees having similar trends of a downward spiral in terms of numbers, it became evident that they too need our help. Planting milkweed and nectar plants is an easy way to give them a helping hand, as well. At the same time, it beautifies our world and ensures a healthy food supply.

I can remember vividly back to 2007, when PM Justin Trudeau was giving a speech near our hometown on the environment. He quoted Einstein who said, "If the **bee** disappeared off the face of the Earth, man would only have four years left to live." Justin was kind enough to pose with our class environmental bear, who donned a butterfly t-shirt, and earrings to match. We named her "Justine Trudeau" in his honour.

Surely this is something to think about! Ecologically, we are linked to many food chains and food webs!

If you don't happen to have your own property to beautify and enhance for pollinators, you can always get involved in a community group that works on projects such as these. Even small planters on balconies can help.

Stratford, Ontario became a Bee City in 2017, dedicated to adopting pollinator friendly practices. In the fall of 2018, funding and plans are in place to begin a Pollinator Pathway along the railway tracks. Trees that will provide food and habitat for pollinators will be planted, which will also beautify the area. Finding otherwise unused land, and filling it with pollinator-friendly plantings makes good sense now to ensure a healthy future for all.

Vision Quest

March 4, 2017

When working on becoming a Reiki master, I was given the name "Painted Turtle Dancer". I found this name odd. I was definitely a butterfly person! I remained open to this given name but it just didn't seem to fit! What it did do, was make me look closely at my identity and see why I was just NOT accepting this new name easily.

One of the activities we did towards the end of the training, was to go off into the woods and meditate. I sat there for an hour or so, breathing in the fresh pine scent of the forest, surrounded by a circle of rocks, I had collected in the morning. It was a chilly, cloudy, autumn day so the forest seemed even darker than usual. All of a sudden, I could feel the sun's rays kissing my cheek. It felt so heavenly and I was pulled towards the nearby lake, like a magnet. I was surprised to see a Monarch above the wet, sandy beach and I started to follow it. Monarchs are not able to fly when it is cool, so it was probably just as happy as I was to see the sunshine. Perhaps it was on its way to Mexico. If it wasn't, it should have been! My shoes sank in the sand, but I just kept moving. My socks were pulled from my feet as I continued running in the direction of the Monarch, in bare feet... but I didn't care. The wet sand felt good as I felt a true connection with the earth and the wondrous butterfly. I made up my mind that I truly wasn't a Painted Turtle Dancer, but a Butterfly Dancer. When the mysterious Monarch flew upwards, towards the robin egg blue sky, I returned to the group confident that I had discovered my true name or at least an additional name.

That morning, when we had gone out to collect rocks that we were drawn to, I seemed to select rocks that had split into two pieces. When I brought mine back to the cottage, I intuitively placed some of them into the shape of a butterfly. The piece that made up the body split into two, so there was now a body and a head. Since that day two more pieces have broken off to make antennae!!

Seeing that butterfly appear from my rockpile, convinced me that I needed a different name. I had been given a name which challenged me, so I would look within and examine who I really was. It strengthened my identity and connection to the butterfly. To this very day, I am grateful for the gift of that name. My rocks, forming the shape of a butterfly, and the other ones I collected that magical day, sit on the shelf beside my bed. reminding me daily of my quest.

Months later, I realized it was more about me learning to speak my truth. A gift in, and of itself. At one time I would have accepted the name politely, despite the turmoil within.

May 11, 2018

I was chatting with a friend about my Reiki names, and she helped me realize that I have many turtle traits as well. And I do! I never rush into anything. I go at my own pace, but when things are flowing like a river, I move forward quickly and easily.

Mark and I dated for seven years and three months before we became engaged. We were married three months later. Then we were married for seven and a half years before Ryan was born. Rachel came along shortly after. Yes, a turtle's pace, I would say!

So rather than change my name, I combined the two. "Painted Turtle and Butterfly Dancer".

When I got home, my friend sent me a photo of a turtle, with a butterfly on its nose. They actually look cute together. Apparently, the butterflies need the minerals found in the turtle's tears. So the turtle is a good companion for the butterfly, and the butterfly attempts to dry the turtle's tears.

Suddenly, I was content with my Reiki name. That night, I found turtle photos Mark had just taken at a nearby nature area on our computer, and in the movie I watched, entitled "Beach House", the characters were conservationists, preserving the turtles on the beach, where they lived. Coincidence? Perhaps.

May 23, 2018

I came across a quote from Dr. Wayne Dyer today.

"When you dance, your purpose is not to get to a certain place on the floor. It's to enjoy each step along the way."

I think this sums up both the turtle and the butterfly quite nicely.

May 23, 2018

Today, I added the above quote while editing this book. Then coincidentally, I got an email from Nature Ontario for "World Turtle Day". It explained that the Painted Turtles that are found in the province of Ontario, are in trouble. as well as all the other turtle species. So as it turns out, "Painted Turtle and Butterfly Dancer" makes more sense now. We must work to protect all of the creatures from man and their actions. Their future and ultimately our own, depend on it.

Often, it takes time before we truly understand why something occurred. I am now at peace with my Reiki name! Look at how long it took me to come to this conclusion !! Perhaps I am a turtle after all.

June 13, 2018

Although I am finished writing this book, I am not finished editing the stories within it. This is what happened this morning.

Out of the corner of my eye, I noticed that one of the "wings" of my rock butterfly, was missing. I questioned Mark, to see if he knew where it was. He didn't know what I was talking about, and I think he even wondered about my sanity. I was absolutely sure there was a logical explanation. Things don't just disappear into thin air, and who would want my rock?

Upon further investigation, I discovered that the rock had fallen off of the shelf and was hiding in my slipper below. I chuckled as I felt relieved that the mystery was solved, even though how it happened, will remain unknown.

I then proceeded to take a closer look at the other rocks I had picked up that day. One looked like a small heart and one was the shape of a rainbow; two of my favourite things. Then, there was a rather ugly large, rock that had split into two. Why I liked it at the time, I do not know. It was heavy and even weighed me down on my quest for just the right rocks, but I refused to part with it.

The final rock I found, that wasn't part of the butterfly, just felt good in my hands and reminded me of an arrow pointing in a direction. I had placed it in front of me while meditating that day, and it actually was pointing in the direction of the beach, where I eventually encountered the Monarch butterfly. When you examine it closely, it looks like a turtle's head.

I looked more carefully at the large rock, thinking why did I even bother to keep it? I had placed it beside the butterfly and it had sat there for a long time. It isn't even attractive in any way, or by any stretch of my imagination, but I just liked it for some strange reason.

I picked the two pieces up in my hands, and mystically I transformed them into a turtle body and head. Using the wings of the butterfly, it became a turtle with its four legs, and the pointed rock became its tail. So now the rocks have transformed into a turtle, with a butterfly on its back, under a rainbow and a heart. Wow! It is starting to all make sense! There goes my imagination again!

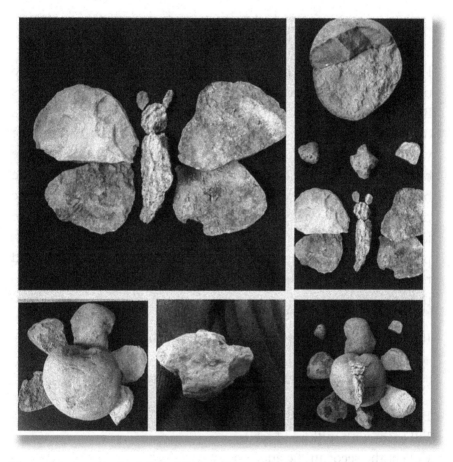

I have been a turtle, hiding from the world. I have now come out of my shell and am free to share my stories. I have a butterfly on my back to dry my tears, love in my heart and although the sun is not always shining, there is a rainbow after every storm.

Butterfly Wishes

March 4, 2017

I truly feel as though I dance with Monarchs. One of my favorite places is the milkweed-filled meadow, near Saint Christopher's Beach, in Goderich, Ontario. I feel lucky when we see Monarchs dancing busily, going about their business without a care in the world, in the Summer. I just love it when the milkweed pods have burst open in the Fall and the seeds are carried off, gently in the breeze. I love making wishes for the butterflies as I help spread the parachuted seeds. Wishes for a safe journey to Mexico. Wishes for lots of milkweed and nectar plants along their path. Wishes for a perfect place for them to overwinter in Mexico, with lots of trees and no snow. Wishes for their numbers to increase, and their return to their former glory.

If you want to help the Monarchs, here is a gift idea.

<u>Milkweed Ornament</u>

Buy empty, clear Christmas tree glass balls.
Fill them with milkweed seeds.
Collect the seeds in the autumn.
Attach a bow to the top and add this poem.

Here are butterfly wishes,
that I picked just for you.
I hope these will help
make lots of dreams come true.

Just hold one in your hand
and gently close your eyes.
Make a special wish
for the Monarch butterflies.
Then blow it into the air
and the wind will do its best.
To harvest a new milkweed plant,
when the seed comes to a rest.
B.Hacking 2004

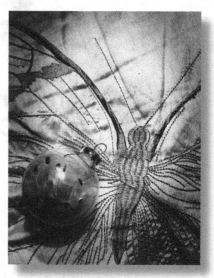

These simple glass ornaments can make a great gift for a bride and groom. While making wishes for their future life together, they can help the Monarchs at the same time. They could also be used as wedding favours, which are especially nice for a Fall wedding.

Milkweed seeds require a period of cold, like they would experience in nature. This process is called cold stratification. You can put the seeds in the refrigerator for a period of a month, before planting them in the Spring, or you can just find milkweed plants in the Fall and help plant the fluffy seeds, by blowing them into the wind.

Children and Butterflies
in the Classroom

March 10, 2017

Raising Monarchs in my classroom for 30 years was definitely a highlight of my career. I never got tired of immersing myself in the excitement of the students, as they experienced Monarch magic.

One September, as my new students entered the classroom, they were greeted with a Monarch eclosing from its chrysalis. Such a perfectly timed occurrence! The butterfly is often seen as a symbol of new beginnings, and it truly was a celebration of the beginning of our year together.

The kids always got a kick out of having their photo taken with a Monarch butterfly on their nose, or as a butterfly barrette in their hair.

They say that when a child learns to love nature, they will grow up protecting what they love. It is my hope that Monarchs will be around for future generations to enjoy. Sure, they will see them on their electronic gadgets, like we see dinosaurs today, however that is just not the same. Not to mention we need them and other pollinators to ensure our food supply.

I firmly believe that a butterfly needs to be released as soon as its wings are dry and it is able to fly, unless the weather isn't cooperating or its wings are damaged. I tried to teach my students the importance of when we remove something from nature, we must return it, unharmed. It's our responsibility to make sure it is cared for properly. I had many kids bring me caterpillars when out on yard duty. I always told them that each caterpillar has a specific food source that it needs. If we don't know what it eats, we should put it back where it was found.

I can remember raising hundreds of Monarchs in September, but when I retired in 2012, only one caterpillar could be found. There were many disappointed teachers that year. It really was an awakening that the Monarchs were in trouble, and we needed to do everything we could to protect them.

I have discovered that children are totally different beings when out in nature. I had a very active group of children the year our school created its Monarch Waystation. In June, the final month of school, we were finished our Ontario provincial testing of reading, writing and math skills. It was a blessing to get outside and work in the dirt, preparing the garden, planting and watering. The kids were amazing, and they loved being outdoors. They were cooperative, on task and excited to be helping the Monarchs. Every once in a while, a Monarch would come along and flutter over the new garden. I'm sure it was smiling and demonstrating its gratitude.

What can children learn from the Monarchs?

They learn that what goes in, must come out. Monarch caterpillars eat a lot of milkweed and therefore excrete a lot of poop! And it's green! This is called frass. I recently met another teacher who also raised Monarchs in the classroom. They had a caterpillar they named Sir Frass-a-Lot. A perfect name for a Monarch caterpillar.

They learn that cycles exist in our world. Seasons, animals, celestial bodies, plants, etc.

They learn that we must protect the habitats of animals. Chopping down the trees on the Monarch mountains, in Mexico, harms their perfect overwintering habitat. Also, that expanding urban areas, take away valuable habitat.

They learn that Monarchs migrate to Mexico to escape our cold, snowy winter. A miraculous feat for such a tiny insect!

They learn that Monarch caterpillars shed their skin (moult) five times as they grow, just like children outgrow their clothes, as they get bigger.

They learn that Monarchs depend on milkweed for nectar, to lay their eggs on, and feed their young.

They learn that milkweed seeds, with the help of their parachutes, travel in the wind to a new location.

They learn that humans can help the environment, but that many of our actions harm it.

Future Son-in-Law Test

March 11, 2017

I knew Jeff was the one for our daughter, Rachel, when the very first Thanksgiving he came home with her, he brought me the most beautiful autumn flowers. It was a sure way to win my heart! Before long he was watching his very first Monarch eclosing from its chrysalis. He demonstrated his patience as he waited for the new butterfly to arrive. The butterfly enjoyed sitting on the gorgeous bouquet as its wings dried. That was Jeff's first butterfly release and I knew it wouldn't be his last… and it wasn't.

Our Hospice

March 11, 2017

I was contacted by the fundraising committee to see if I could provide one hundred Monarchs for a special butterfly release, to raise money for the Hospice being built in our community. Their symbol is a butterfly, as it represents the transformation from this life into the next. A butterfly is an excellent symbol as it transitions from one stage to the next, gracefully.

There would be nothing that I would like better than to have one hundred Monarchs to release all at one time, however, I had to tell them that I hadn't even seen one hundred Monarchs, in total, here in the past five years. When it comes to butterflies, it is hard to predict how many butterflies you will have at any given time, especially when the population has shown a decline in recent years. At all cost, the butterflies' safety must be taken into consideration.

I hope this summer there will be lots of Monarchs!

Monarch Parade

March 13, 2017

Before our school had its own butterfly garden, (September, 2004) and when there were many Monarch butterflies, the primary classes at Avon School made Monarch wings out of pizza boxes. We "flew" down to the Shakespearean Gardens, which is loaded with a collection of gorgeous pollinator flowers. Gathered in a large circle, each class released their Monarchs chanting, "Off you go to Mexico!" A TV crew was there to capture the glorious orange and black wings fluttering upwards, over the children's heads and away into the clear, blue sky. How Monarchs know which way to go to Mexico is just one of the great mysteries associated with these magnificent creatures. No one can say for sure. Is it an innate ability, magnetism, or Monarch magic at work again?

It was the first day at our school for Riley Brathwaite. She and her family had come to stay with her grandparents because their home in Grenada had been damaged during the category 5 hurricane Ivan, which devastated their island. She was put in charge of releasing the butterflies for our class and Riley recalls being excited, while at the same time being nervous because everything was so new to her. The Monarchs were a link between her new home and the one she had left behind, as there were Monarchs in Grenada as well. We wondered if they had survived the hurricane. Winds can be beneficial for Monarchs as they migrate, however winds that are too strong can be detrimental or devastating.

When the students returned to the school, they were extremely tired. As we rested on the front steps, we imagined how tired the Monarchs must be on their 2500 mile (4000 kilometre) migration to Mexico from Stratford, Ontario, Canada. We had only travelled a short distance each way. Monarch butterfly-shaped cookies quickly restored our energy after a busy afternoon.

Mariposa Monarca

March 13, 2017

Shortly after the Monarch parade of children, I dropped in on my friend Sue's "Teddy Bear Shop" in Shakespeare, Ontario. Sue possesses a rare talent for transforming well loved fur coats into the most adorable Teddy bears ever, each with a personality of its very own.

She had seen the Monarchs being released on TV and asked what my class would be doing for excitement, now that the butterflies were gone. I really didn't have an answer to that question. Sue quickly changed that, by presenting my class with the cutest bear ever! She made us promise to give "Harrison" lots of love and adventures. He had sat on her shelf at the store, for a couple of years. People would pick him up, give him a squeeze but no one had given him his "forever" home.

Little did I know then, that Harrison would travel the world, meet the Prime Minister, dry children's tears, and become such an important part of our class. We learned so much from his travels and he certainly restored imagination, which seems to be often lacking in childhood these days with the Internet taking over. Perhaps it was the "Harrison Project", that elevated my imagination to an all time high.

One of Harrison's first trips was with me to the Monarchs' overwintering grounds, in Mexico. He was renamed Mariposa Monarca which means Monarch Butterfly, in Spanish. He was adorned with his own pair of wings and "pipe cleaner" antennae. Traveling with other Canadian and American teachers was exciting and certainly reinforced the idea that Canada, United States and Mexico need to work together to rescue the declining Monarch population. Harrison certainly brought smiles to those people he encountered… and a smile is the same in any language. Harrison was photographed with the Monarchs on the mountains, and his journal helped make my trip come alive for my students. Traveling with a cute, little bear certainly made the trip even more fun and internationally converging…

Our first visit to El Rosario Monarch Butterfly Reserve.

Mariposa Monarca has traveled with me to the Mexican mountains each time. He especially enjoyed meeting Sara Dykman from the Butterbike Project (www.beyondabook.com), before she began following the Monarchs' migration from Mexico, through the United States, up to Canada and back down to Mexico again, on her bike. Mariposa Monarca presented Sara with her own bear, complete with Monarch wings, that would keep her company on her long journey. She named him Mariposita (little butterfly) and he was sewn under her bicycle seat. I can hardly wait to hear of their adventures when Sarah visits Stratford, in August.

A Visit from Beyond???

March 13, 2017

When I was raising Monarchs in the classroom, I just loved to do a butterfly release out in the front garden so parents, as well a siblings could participate in this awesome experience.

I'll never forget the day a Monarch flew up and over the school after being released and then circled back, landing on a toddler in a stroller. The butterfly looked like it came back to kiss her cheek. It stayed for quite a while, crawled to her head, looking like a butterfly barrette in her fine golden hair, and then it was off. I watched in awe as the young child took it all in stride. She just let it happen. I couldn't help but wonder if her dear grandfather, who had been our principal, had something to do with it?? He had passed away one weekend before she was born, at the age of 52. It was such a shock to the school community!

In movies, they often use a butterfly to represent someone's spirit who has passed on. Who knows? Perhaps it works that way in real life too! How can one ever prove it?

What Animal Speaks To You???
(Donna's Dragonfly)

March 13, 2017

For me, butterflies have woven themselves in and out of the tapestry of my life. I've always marvelled at how they come to me, in the most interesting ways. I am surprised but then again, I'm not. I just smile and say thank you for yet another miracle. I caution people, whom I give caterpillars to, that they may just get caught up in the Monarch magic too!… and usually, I'm right!

For other people, they may connect with other members of the animal kingdom. I have heard many stories about cardinals, dogs, cats, owls, elephants, blue herons, etc. that speak to people in some mystical way.

September, 2016.

One day a mysterious dragonfly showed up in my life. I was walking through one of the most beautiful gardens here in Stratford, on my way to work. The Shakespearean Gardens!

Out of the corner of my eye I saw a turquoise and black dragonfly, sitting on an eye level tree branch. Curiously, I put my hand out to it, and it crawled onto my hand as if it had been waiting for me to give it a ride. I was able to admire it more closely. It was adorned in jewel-like hues and seemed to be at peace with the world.

I offered to release my little hitchhiker upon the beautiful florals surrounding us but it was quite content to stay with me. Perhaps, it was trying to camouflage itself against the turquoise and black outfit I was wearing. We seemed to match! It traveled to the downtown area with me, and it could have flown off at any moment, but it chose not to.

I paused at the garden in front of our City Hall and tried to convince it that this was the perfect place for a dragonfly, but it didn't agree. It clung to me like a terrified child on the first day of school.

Finally, we arrived at the ladies' store where I worked. The store was unusually quiet and it was just the dragonfly and me. I must say, I enjoyed being with my new found friend. I couldn't help but feel I was holding it for someone else, but for whom I was not sure.

This exquisite creature showed me it's amazing colours under the magnification of my cell phone's camera! It made an excellent photographic model.

Before long, a lady named Lois came into the store. I introduced her to my new friend. She quickly said, "Oh! That's Donna!", as if it was no surprise.

Perplexed, I asked, "Donna?"

Apparently she had a friend pass away from cancer many years ago, and before she died she said she was going to come back as a dragonfly. So Donna's family and friends see dragonflies in unusual, unexpected places and they are no longer surprised at these occurrences.

Who would expect to find a dragonfly waiting for your arrival, at a clothing store?

I photographed the dragonfly with this lovely lady and she was going to share this experience with Donna's family. As soon as the photo shoot was finished, the dragonfly flew out of the open door. It didn't fly around the store trying to find its escape route. It knew exactly where it was going, and it's mission was accomplished.

I looked at the photos when I got home, and I noticed that Lois had a butterfly on her dress... and the dragonfly had a butterfly on its thorax. The next customer that came into the store had a dragonfly on her outfit. The first customer of the following day had a dragonfly on her jacket, both front and back. I just smiled!

In March, 2017, Lois came into the store. I hadn't seen her since our dragonfly encounter, six months earlier. I happened to be working on this book and asked her if I could read her the story, about Donna. I wanted to see if her perception of that event matched mine...and it did. As I finished reading the story, she looked at me with tears in her eyes, and you'll never guess what Lois said ???, "Today is the anniversary of Donna's passing."

I hadn't seen Lois since that glorious September day when we shared those precious moments, with the dragonfly who came for a visit. Donna had brought us together once again! That day I told her about Chantelle's wish to come back as a butterfly, if she didn't survive her surgery. No sooner did Lois leave the store, when Chantelle appeared outside the store window. I invited Chantelle in to tell her about this strange morning.

That is not the last time I heard Donna's name. I was telling my friend, Ev about the mysterious visit from the dragonfly. She remembered an incident one summer, when she was vacationing in Newfoundland with several women. They were outside, and a dragonfly joined them. They too, took photos of this tame creature. One of the ladies just happened to have been a friend of Donna's, and she too believed that Donna had something to do with this special visit. There just has to be something more to life after death. Donna gives us hope that this is so.

So it appears that one must be open to miracles, and take the time to see the events around them. I was reminded that although butterflies miraculously show up in my life, I should be open to other animal messengers as well.

This occurrence took me back in time. One day, I was out on yard duty when a dragonfly landed on my face. The students were extremely excited, and luckily I had my camera. It was wonderful to get a close up and personal look at this flying insect. The students were even learning lessons out on the playground. Our school has been dedicated to creating a wonderful outdoor classroom, so that valuable lessons can happen, even at recess.

The Future

March 17, 2017

I remain optimistic and envision a world where all species interrelate, prosper and thrive.

In Canada, the best thing we can do to protect the Monarch butterfly species is to plant milkweed and keep the plants chemical-free. Up until the spring of 2014, it was classified as a noxious weed. With declining Monarch populations, it was recognized that this was part of the problem. It was taken off the noxious weed list, at least in the Canadian province of Ontario. Now, we must change the way we think about this magnificent plant, the only food source for the Monarch caterpillar. As I've said before, I prefer to call it milkflower because it possesses the most beautiful blooms with an exquisite scent. I'm sure it was no accident that Mother Nature created it that way. Monarchs must be able to detect its sweet nectar from afar, so they can find it to lay their precious eggs. Many pollinators love this plant!

By planting our gardens with pollinators in mind, we can be part of the solution. There are many types of native milkweed which can add beauty to your garden while attracting Monarchs and other pollinators, as well. Nectar plants are also necessary to nourish adult butterflies. Check out your local nursery and look for these plants that will help our pollinators.

You can even get your garden certified by Monarch Watch as a Way Station, which serves as a nectaring and resting spot along the migratory route, as well as a breeding habitat throughout the summer months. Be sure to check out their website! (http:www.monarchwatch.org) Wouldn't it be great to have these special places all along the migration route from Canada to the mountains in Mexico?

On Canada Day, July 1, 2016, Prime Minister Justin Trudeau, President Barack Obama and Mexican President Pena Nietzsche, promised to create a butterfly highway along the Monarch's migration pathway. Hopefully this will become a reality in the near future.

It is also important to keep your garden as natural as possible, by including plants native to your area, and free of herbicides and pesticides.

By helping our butterflies and bees, we are also helping ourselves. If we take care of nature, nature will take care of us.

Let's do everything we can to ensure that that these simple pleasures are there for future generations.

What we do for the butterflies...we do for the bees.
What we do for the bees...we do for all pollinators.
What we do for all pollinators...we do for humans.
What we do for humans… we do for our children.
What we do for our children...we do for the future.

Celebrating a Loved One's Life

March 17, 2017

It is always hard to lose someone we love, especially when they are so young.

Friends had lost their child, tragically. It was autumn and how I wished that I had a chrysalis to give them! That year, Monarchs were very scarce. In fact, the population had reached their lowest numbers ever.

I was walking through a garden center and happened to find a chrysalis hidden among the many plants. I asked if I could have it for this grieving family and they were happy to let me take it.

A couple weeks later, I had this voice inside, urging me to make a special supper for our friends. When I delivered it, I said that I had this feeling that we should be celebrating. I didn't know what, but this thought would just not go away. The father smiled and went to get the newly eclosed Monarch. Now that was something to celebrate! We took the butterfly outside to release it, as its wings were dry, and just at that moment, the Snowbirds (three stunt planes getting ready for an airshow) flew over our heads. It definitely was a celebration as the family released the Monarch in memory of their loved one.

Catching Monarch Magic

March 17, 2017

Well here I am at the end of the journal that I had won. Coincidentally, the story that I'm writing on the last page belongs to Dee, the person responsible for the catalyst that sent my dream into reality.(this journal!) I thought perhaps the writing would be complete when I got to the end, but apparently that is not the case. The story didn't fit the small space that was left, and there are still more stories to tell.

When I give an interested person a caterpillar, I warn them that they probably will catch Monarch "fever" and that they should be open to the magical nature of this marvellous insect.

I had given one to my friends, Rob and Dee. They fondly named it Mona Lisa and enjoyed watching its transformation. Well, Mona Lisa turned out to be a boy.

*Name change = <u>Man</u>a Lisa

How does one tell?

A male has a black dot on each of its bottom wings(top) . A female does not, and also has thicker, black veins and abdomen (bottom).

My students were always delighted to share that fact with their parents and any other classroom visitor. When a butterfly eclosed, they waited excitedly to discover what sex it was, and were proud of themselves if their predictions were correct.

Rob and Dee sent Mana Lisa on its way. They watched as he perched on a tree and then flew over their heads and was gone. At least they thought so!

March 18, 2017

A few days later I received a call from Rob. I could detect the excitement in his voice. He had just returned home from driving Dee to the airport. Within a few blocks of home, a Monarch butterfly appeared out of nowhere and was flying around the interior of Rob's car. Where did it come from? Was it Mana Lisa? The windows were closed so how did it get in? Monarch magic? Perhaps!

Dee and Rob continue to learn about the Monarchs' amazing life cycle and migration habits. Just this morning Dee received a lesson on what happens to the Monarchs after spending their winter huddled together on the Oyamel fir trees at the top of Mexico's mountains.

When the temperature is cool/cold (less than 55 degrees F or 13 degrees C) and the sun is not shining, you will see huge clusters of Monarchs squeezed tightly together. The Oyamel canopy and the warmth of the tree trunks, protect the Monarchs until spring. That is why it is important to preserve the forests on these mountains.

In the spring, as the temperatures rise, the Monarchs will fly off of the trees looking for nectar and water. Lately, the Monarchs have been seen flying throughout the winter, as the temperatures have been warmer than usual. Could this be an example of global warming?

In the spring, they will mate, which is an interesting sight to see. The male will fly on top of the female and then lift her off into the air. They stay conjoined for many hours. I have only witnessed this once, here in Canada.

Many of the males die right there in Mexico and the females fly up to Texas to deposit their eggs on the flourishing milkweed. They too will die, and it is their offspring that will continue their northern migration. It is often said it is the great grandchildren that come to visit us in Canada.

That's why ensuring that there is lots of milkweed planted along the migration route is so critical. Nectar plants to provide energy and nourishment, is just as important. Many projects are being undertaken to make this happen. Monarchs need milkweed as they move northward for reproduction, and nectar plants as they move southward to Mexico.

Dee and Rob have their special Monarch nursery ready for when they return to Canada. Rob surprised Dee one day with a trip to the Cambridge Butterfly Conservatory, here in Ontario. Dee was in her glory! Dee's goal for this year was to see a female lay an egg in the wild and raise it so she could experience the entire life cycle.

After seeing the movie "Patch Adams", Dee was amazed to see the butterfly and she too wished she could have one land on her. It was delightful to make that happen. The Monarch truly enjoyed being with Dee. So much so it didn't want to leave her. Dee is one special lady, so I can't say I blame it.

Organically Grown Butterflies

March 17, 2017

I received an email one day from a fellow Monarch enthusiast. We exchanged many of our experiences online and I knew I needed to visit his organic farm located not too far away. Monarchs were few and far between that year, but this fellow's property was a haven for the Monarchs, and they had found it.

When I got there, I was greeted by this fine young teenager. I asked for his dad, thinking that was who I had been communicating with. I was pleasantly surprised to discover this young man was indeed who I was looking for. It's always great to see our young people caring for the world around them. We hopped on his four wheeler and went off to explore the many Monarch habitats both he and nature had created. It was a year where I hadn't seen many Monarchs, so it was wonderful observing them enjoying this glorious oasis.

The next time I visited the teen, his dad was very ill. We decided it would be great for him to have his own caterpillar to watch as he lay in bed. There is nothing like the marvel of watching this miraculous transformation. Before long, his dad passed away. Such a sad time, especially for someone so young.

He told me the story of coming out of his house after hearing the news and seeing a Monarch lingering around. It gave him comfort. We are reminded of the "Butterfly's Promise" and that his dad was now free, to fly away from his pain and suffering.

Shortly thereafter, he and I paid a visit to Greenway Garden Center to meet John Powers and Donald Davis, both Monarch mentors, and my friend was selected to release the butterflies.

June 11, 2018

His family has put in a nature trail in front of their country store called the "Organic Oasis", which is a perfect name for a pollinator-friendly location. It has an enclosure where visitors are able to observe the Monarch's miraculous metamorphosis. Sharing this phenomenon, will help educate others in this gorgeous natural setting, free of pesticides. (https://organicoasis.on.ca/)

Butterfly Dreams

March 18, 2017

Every autumn our two children, Ryan and Rachel, were immersed in the searching for, and rearing of Monarch caterpillars for my classroom.

During the summer holidays, we were always delighted to see a female Monarch laying her eggs as she danced from one milkweed plant to another. Carefully, we would collect the eggs and keep them safe until they were butterflies, ready to be released.

The Monarchs encouraged us to spend time together as a family, hiking trails and enjoying being in nature. The lessons were plentiful, teaching us about life, death, the environment, as well as so many other things. They inspired us to write about them and work to protect them.

Speeches, poems, books and songs.

When Rachel was eight, she wrote a simple poem about butterflies entitled, "Butterfly Dreams". It ended up becoming a song set to music by Berthold Carriere, the music director of Stratford's Shakespearean Festival. That song traveled to New York City and Ottawa with the St. Mary's Children's Choir. It sounded just like a butterfly flitting about in the garden. The day the choir left to go to New York City, to sing Rachel's song, a teacher on our staff had a Swallowtail butterfly eclose in her classroom. She didn't know what to do with it since it was January here in Canada, so she sent it home with my son, Ryan. We thought it was amazing that a butterfly would find its way into our home, as Rachel's song was about to be launched. I guess Butterfly Dreams really do come true! Even in January!

Ryan wrote his speech one year educating others about the mysteries of the Monarchs. Those were in the days when they were plentiful. I can't help but wonder what he would say now. Things have changed drastically since then.

Wishes For the Monarchs

March 18, 2017

One glorious Fall day, my class was out for a hike. White "cotton candy" clouds filled the blue sky as the sun peeked down, caressing the children's faces. We arrived at a meadow filled with wildflowers, including milkweed, preparing for winter. I just love it when the seed pods pop open, revealing the hundreds of treasures inside. Each seed can produce a new plant for the Monarchs. Each seed can ensure the Monarchs' future. Each seed was a teacher that day, giving lessons the students would never forget.

The kids absolutely loved dancing around, releasing the seeds into the gentle Autumn breeze. They were happy and free; the seeds and the children! This is the way childhood should be! I absolutely loved watching them!

They inspired me to write about the unbelievable power of a tiny milkweed seed and the miracle within.

Butterfly Wishes

This is a butterfly wish, also known as a milkweed seed. Blow it into the air and with the help of its "parachute", the wind will carry it to a new home. Make a wish!

It will rest on the soil under the snow, for the long cold winter. In the spring, the seed will grow roots, deep into the sun warmed earth. A stem will shoot up towards the sun, dressed in fresh green leaves.

A Monarch mother will usually lay an egg on the underside of the milkweed leaf and like an umbrella, the leaf will protect it from the wind and the rain. Three to five days later, a teeny, tiny caterpillar will hatch out and eat its first meal; its egg shell! Knowing that her baby will need lots of milkweed to eat, she usually only lays one egg per plant. Mama Monarchs have been known to lay 500 eggs!!

During the next ten to fourteen days, the caterpillar will eat nothing but milkweed leaves. Its weight will multiply almost 3000 times. It will grow and shed its skin (moult), five times. When it's ready, the caterpillar will walk about until it finds a suitable place to hang. It will spin a silky, white button and hang upside down in a "J" shape.

Its skin will split open and it will become an exquisite jewel-like green chrysalis adorning what looks like a shimmering gold necklace. Its antenna, head cap and legs will fall off, as they are no longer needed. For the next 10 to 14 days, many changes will happen inside the chrysalis and a complete transformation will take place.

Suddenly the outer shell will become transparent and you will see the orange, black and white wings peeking through. The chrysalis will split open and the butterfly will eclose upside down. It will use its legs to cling to the hollow shell. Its abdomen will be huge, filled with fluid which will be pumped into the wings over the next few minutes. The wings will grow larger and fuller.

How did that butterfly fit inside that tiny chrysalis?

The wings will dry and begin to move back and forth; back and forth! Soon it will take its first flight. Up, up and away!

Without milkweed, there will be no Monarchs.
So, make lots of milkweed wishes so Monarchs can flourish.

The Life Cycle
Of the
Monarch Butterfly

The Amazing Marvelous Metamorphosis

March 18, 2017

Teaching children about the amazing transformation a Monarch goes through in its lifetime, was one of my favourite lessons to teach to my amazed primary grade pupils. From egg, to caterpillar, to chrysalis, to butterfly… and then the cycle begins again.

When our daughter, Rachel was quite young, she didn't find the transition to be so thrilling. She had named her caterpillar "Tickles" and enjoyed watching it munch on the milkweed. She was virtually inconsolable when she discovered that Tickles had gone missing. How could that green thing hanging inside the container be Tickles?

I was never so happy to see a Monarch eclose in my life! It was the longest two weeks ever!

Rachel was delighted with the butterfly but then we had a new problem…she didn't want to see it go.

That lead me to write the children's story "Tickle's Surprise", so all was not lost!

When raising Monarchs, we always released the butterfly as soon as its wings were dry, unless the weather conditions did not allow it (high winds, rain,etc.). Rachel soon understood the importance of releasing the butterflies so they could fly free. Each year, we remind Rachel of her pet, Tickles and smile.

Rachel happily releasing Tickles.

Finding Balance

March 18, 2017

A butterfly is beautifully symmetrical and it is perfectly balanced, as it takes to flight. Its intricately designed wings help it maneuver the many miles/kilometres it must travel, as it makes its way to its winter home in Mexico or when migrating North. They are delicate, but strong.

Occasionally, a butterfly's wings fail to "pump up" after it first ecloses. That's when the butterfly becomes a pet and must be cared for. Last year, my friend Mary was raising Monarchs in her kindergarten class. One of their butterflies did not develop properly. It was a lesson for the children that although not perfect, it was still going to be okay. It returned to me, and "Tiny" lived out it's life nestled among scented blossoms and feeding on orange slices. It enjoyed sitting on my finger and it was sad to see him die a few weeks later. It was a lesson about differences and disabilities. Although Tiny lived its' life differently than other Monarchs, it was still valued and loved.

A butterfly demonstrates how important balance is. A wing that is broken or misshapen can make flying difficult, or impossible.

Balance is important in our own lives, too. Balancing work and play, work and family, family and self-care, and the list goes on. The older I get, the more I realize how important achieving balance is, in all areas of our lives.

Many years ago, scientists were developing migratory tags for butterfly wings. It was difficult creating a tag, small and light enough, as to not throw off the Monarch's delicately balanced wings, especially when it needed to travel a great distance. The tag must be able to endure many weather conditions, as well. These recorded tags help scientists, by showing where a butterfly had been released from, and where it has migrated to, as well as the person who tagged it.

Donald Davis, of Toronto, holds the Guinness World Record for a tagged butterfly that flew the furthest distance. He released a butterfly in Presqu'ile Provincial Park near Brighton, Ontario, Canada on September 10, 1988. It was discovered in Austin, Texas, on April 8, 1989. That's 2880 miles, or a whopping 4635 kilometers. Donald's butterfly proved that the tag did not hinder the butterfly's ability to travel during its migration from Canada. This butterfly had probably flown to Mexico for the winter and was heading back northward, 7 months later !!! Donald should be commended for tagging Monarchs since 1988, and he continues to this day.

John G. Powers and Donald Davis

Last month, while visiting the Monarch mountains, I had the pleasure of meeting Terry Whitman, Betty McCulloch and Katherine Haughton who tag Monarchs, near Toronto. They were in Mexico to meet the man who found one of their butterflies at El Rosario Butterfly Reserve. How exciting for them! The Monarch was even alive when the tag was discovered.

The Butterfly Man®

March 22, 2017

Before the Internet, we had real people for mentors. We still can have them, however mentors are now often found online, and you rarely have the chance or need to meet them in person. Google has often replaced people, for answering questions that we have.

John G. Powers served as our family's mentor when our children were growing up, as he is a wealth of information about butterflies. Whenever we had a question, he eagerly shared his passion and knowledge with us. His love for butterflies of all kinds began as a young boy, when his Dad gave him a butterfly net. While other kids were spending their money on hockey cards, John was able to interact with nature at the local park, for free. It makes me wonder if John's passion for insects would be the same if he had been born today. Our children need to be out in the great outdoors and experience all that it has to offer. Over the years, John has connected thousands of children to nature, with the many kits he has created specifically for that purpose. He certainly was a huge influence on our own children over the years. John taught us the art of tagging and maintaining the Monarch's delicate wing balance in the process. Our family especially enjoyed visiting with John during his Monarch Days® each September, when he educated people about the glorious migration, by giving them the opportunity to release their own tagged Monarch.

John had a dream to create a butterfly conservatory. My mother heard him speak, loved his idea and cheerfully bought each person in our family a membership to help his vision become a reality. John's dream started in his basement! There he readily accepted visitors who enjoyed seeing his fantastic collection of butterflies, stick bugs, beetles and all the other interesting items he had collected since 1959, worldwide. From there, he built a large greenhouse which housed many butterfly species from all over the world. His dream kept growing as he received funding to build Wings of Paradise® Butterfly Conservatory; a 25,000 square foot building. His dream had come true, but often dreams change and John moved his valuable collection to Greenway Garden Center, a nursery specializing in pollinator plants.

Our daughter, Rachel visiting Wings of Paradise with my Mom and Dad. Notice the butterfly on my Mom's shoulder.

For over 45 years, John has shared his passion with his Incredible World of Bugs and Flying Jewels® exhibit and continues to educate and motivate others. His spectacular collection has travelled from coast to coast many times, and it has fascinated millions. It is no wonder that he is known as The Butterfly Man®, standing out in a crowd with his brightly coloured, butterfly shirts.

In September, 2005, John released tagged Monarchs for the 100th anniversary of a local church. Each butterfly's tag contained a teeny-tiny bible quote. In March, 2006, one of the tagged Monarchs was found on the mountains in Mexico. The quote it was adorned with was, "With God, all things are possible."(Mark 10:27, KJV) A very appropriate message for a butterfly that was able to migrate all the way to its overwintering grounds, from Canada. It truly is an amazing achievement requiring courage, strength, endurance and probably a few miracles along the way.

Our son, Ryan, donated a Monarch that never lost its head cap during its metamorphosis from a caterpillar into a butterfly, to John's collection. The butterfly had failed to cast off its head cap when entering the chrysalis stage and as a result it had no proboscis to drink nectar, and no antennae. It enjoyed basking in the sunshine on our screen door. Even though it was unable to eat, it surprised us by living for quite a few weeks.

You could call John the person, with some of the most amazing collections in the world. His autograph collection contains over 100 songs with the word butterfly in them, signed by the artists, including "Butterfly Dreams" signed by our daughter, Rachel. His stamp collection contains blocks, sheets and postmarked stamps from every Capitol City in the world. His newest collection and exhibit, is called Banknotes and Butterflies® and contains money adorned with butterflies from all over the world. John is the only person I know who can say the word "butterfly" in every language. Wow!

The most miraculous thing about John's collections are that he has done everything without a computer, or the internet. The only way to contact John is by phone, by "snail" mail, or in person. He was able to make contacts in over 100 countries throughout the world by handing out business cards! John has proven that the personal touch works and it has served him well, right up to this day.

Peace

March 19, 2017

I woke up this morning thinking about the importance of finding peace in our lives. Oh, to be like a butterfly. So calm.

It is stressful, constantly dealing with conflict. We, as humans are not always going to agree, so we need to find ways to deal with issues peacefully, so we don't intensify the situation at hand.

The poem "The Peaceful Butterfly" was written many years ago, but it's message holds true today. I can remember that the last verse did not come until weeks after the rest was written. It is the most important. So often we hold on to grudges from the past. In order to truly be free, we must forgive. It doesn't mean we like what a person did, it just means we are able to move on. We no longer are going to allow another person or their actions, to control our lives. Forgiveness takes us back to where we were before the encounter.

Persistence

March 19, 2017

It is persistence that helps us achieve our goals.

A Monarch demonstrates persistence, time and time again…

- when it dances inside its egg and finally escapes
- when it continues to eat milkweed for its entire caterpillar life
- when it walks about until it finds the perfect place to hang in a "J"
- when it splits open its skin to reveal the chrysalis within
- when it struggles to eclose from its chrysalis
- when it clings to the empty chrysalis so it can dry its wings perfectly
- when it flies many thousands of miles/kilometres braving rain, wind, cars, etc. to make it all the way to the mountains in Mexico, to survive the winter
- when it huddles together with other treemates to stay warm and conserve energy, to endure the winter before mating in the spring
- when a female flies to Texas to lay her eggs before her life comes to an end
- when she searches for milkweed to lay her eggs on, especially when mankind sprays the milkweed, to eradicate it

Each and every time, its persistence allows it to reach its goals. Persistence pays off!

Contentment
(Being Happy in the Moment)

March 19, 2017

There is something to be said about being content with the present moment. As a butterfly flies around a garden, it appears happy. I'm sure it's not worrying about the past or thinking about the future.

The past is over, but often we let it dictate the way we feel today. This is a choice. It's not always easy to let go, but doing so, is freeing.

Often we feel we will be happy when a certain event in our life occurs. Again, this is a conscious choice. We can be happy now, with where we are, with what we have, and with who we are.

The Metamorphosing
Title of this Book

March 22, 2017

In the middle of the night, I woke up thinking that the title to this book should be "When a Butterfly Whispers" rather than "When a Butterfly Speaks."

We will see what happens!

More on Mentors -Ted Blowes

March 22, 2017

During the course of a lifetime we have many mentors, from parents, to siblings, to teachers, to friends. According to the Oxford dictionary, "a mentor is an experienced and trusted advisor." Just before I retired from teaching, I was lucky enough to have Ted Blowes (affectionately known as Mr. Stratford) come into my life. He had been our mayor in Stratford, Ontario for 10 years, a former geography teacher, and on just about every committee there was, not only to make Stratford the beautiful place it is today, but the World. He had suggested that I join our city's "Communities in Bloom" committee. I laughed and said I would love to, but when I retired. Well, if you happened to know Ted, he didn't readily accept the word "no", so, although I was busy as a primary teacher, I squeezed CIB in. It turned out to be one of the best decisions of my life, opening more doors than I had ever thought possible. It was the key to my life on the other side of the school door. The people I've met have been incredible and I have learned so much. I have had the pleasure of traveling throughout Canada and seeing this beautiful country that we live in.

When Ted turned 75, I unfortunately missed the big celebration, but promised him a Sushi lunch and a trip to the Greenway Garden Center. We were going to select pollinator plants to beautify one of the Community Living houses, for people with intellectual/physical challenges. Ted had an incredible way of turning a celebration for him, into something for the community.

Now apparently Ted was a picky eater, but I think he rather enjoyed the new dining experience at my favourite restaurant, complete with deep fried ice cream and a birthday candle. If he didn't, he certainly disguised it well.

After lunch, we picked out aromatic pollinator plants and visited John Powers' collection and the butterfly greenhouse. We were inspired by the beautiful pollinator garden shaped like a butterfly. Ted smiled as a butterfly landed on his shoulder and moved to his face.

The day was not yet over, after we returned to Stratford. We had a garden to plant and plant we did! Before we were done, we had attracted our first Monarch and again a picture to prove it. I think that's the moment that Ted had captured "Monarch magic".

Before long, Ted had the city plant its first pollinator garden under the Confederation Bridge between Stratford's Shakespearean Festival Theater and the Art Gallery. Ted had a way of getting things done! He believed in giving back to his community, and taking care of our environment. He understood that Monarch butterflies and other pollinators, were in trouble. Milkweed was not planted in this garden, as it was at that time, considered to be a noxious weed.

In June 2012, I retired a year early from the career that I truly loved! Ted had shown me that there was life beyond the classroom door. I kidded Ted, about being my mentor for retirement, and he took that role very seriously. We met often, as he introduced me to the world of retirement and volunteerism. When we traveled to Toronto to man the National Communities in Bloom booth at "Canada Blooms", Ted eagerly chatted with the booth next to us, discussing plans for yet another garden for Stratford.

Unfortunately, Ted passed away May 11, 2013 in his 76th year.

Tears flow down my cheeks as I remember what a devastating day that was for Stratford, and his family, who so graciously shared him with his community that he loved.

Ted's friends gathered a week later at the Eileen Langley Community Living building to plant two more pollinator gardens. Ted had been an active visitor there. That Summer, when the Communities in Bloom judges visited that building, a single Monarch butterfly danced among those gardens and flew off into the blue sky, as soon as it was sure it had been seen by the judges.

Ted Blowes left this world far too soon, with work left to be done. He also left this world with many friends who still to this day, are ensuring that his visions become a reality. Projects include snowflake lights along the Avon river, planting red and white tulips for the 150th birthday of Canada and a new pollinator garden in his memory, that will educate and hopefully motivate others to protect our world and all living things. The original pollinator garden that the city planted is turning into a much larger butterfly shaped garden, as I write.

I am just so thankful for the time I was privileged to have, with Ted. I shared my passion for butterflies with him and he helped me realize that this passion was a gift to treasure. If I hadn't retired early, I wouldn't have had the opportunity to learn, grow and ease into retirement the way I did, with Ted by my side. Ted taught with his whole being, and his actions, not only with his words.

As they say, when the student is ready, the teacher appears. Well, Ted appeared as I was transforming from a teacher, back to being a student.

Serenity Rescues a Moth

March 22, 2017

My little friend, seven year old Serenity and I were shopping one day. While I was talking to the sales clerk, Serenity espied a moth tangled in a spider's web. I don't know how she ever saw it as it was under a shelf, at floor level. We gently broke the web around it without hurting its delicate wings, in the process. We brushed off the remaining web that clung to the poor little thing. Then we took it out and placed it in one of the boulevard gardens. Moths are nocturnal, so it quickly said thank you and crawled under a leaf, away from the sunlight. We probably don't think about moths very much, as they come out after dark. They are not as visible as butterflies in our world, but just as important.

The Moth's Surprise

March 22, 2017

One day some students brought me this beautiful burgundy and gray moth that they had found on our playground. We assumed it was dead as it laid perfectly still. I put it in my wooden butterfly box to show it to my students, and then took it home to have Mark identify it for me. It was a Blinded Sphinx Moth.

That night around 10 o'clock, after the sun had set, I heard a strange sound coming from the wooden box. It was the moth which had woken up! What a surprise!

The next morning, we had an even bigger surprise! She had gifted us with about 100 eggs. Now we needed to know what type of food to get for the caterpillars, when the eggs hatched. More research was needed. We consulted with others on Facebook and quickly had the answers we were looking for. We freed the moth, but kept her eggs. Many of them hatched, but they needed to pupate underground. We found the perfect spot and released the caterpillars back into nature so that they could burrow into the dirt, before emerging as adult moths. I learn something new every day!

When You Plant for Pollinators, They Will Come

March 22, 2017

Fryfogel Inn and Tavern is a historical building located just outside of Shakespeare, Ontario. In recent years, the Historical Society had been restoring the Inn. To beautify the property, an arboretum was created. Hearing that pollinators were endangered, 2200 plants were added to further make good use of this land. It is now a registered Monarch Way Station.

One day, I was late for a meeting being held at the Inn. I parked my car and as I headed for the Inn, I thought I was about to be attacked by a bat, as I felt something swooping above my head. Boy, was I surprised to see a pair of mating Monarchs. The male attaches to the female and carries her off into the air. This pair landed on a nearby tree branch and they paused there long enough for me to go inside, interrupt the meeting, and bring the board members outside to see this rare sight. Their garden was doing exactly what they had hoped it would! We quickly photographed this exciting act of nature for the local newspapers! This was the first time I had seen a mating pair in Canada. When doing a Monarch presentation, I was telling the audience that mating Monarchs are a common sight on the mountains of Mexico, which are 10,000 feet high. One clever man intervened with the comment, "I guess they are members of the TWO-Mile High Club". We all broke out in laughter.

Barbara J. Hacking

A special thank you to Reg White, who recognized that pollinators were in trouble and Jane Eligh-Feryn for designing, planning and creating a wonderful garden with lots of pollinator protecting plants. Many Arboretum committee members were involved in its creation, as well. This garden helps educate the many visitors to the site, including school children who visit the Inn for Pioneer Days.

During the years when Monarchs were a rare sight, it was usually in a garden containing pollinator plants, that you would see them. It reminds me how important these gardens are.

Swallowtail Sunday

March 23, 2017

One sunny Sunday afternoon, Mark and I were visiting my brother Bruce, and his wife Linda. As we sat on their back deck, we noticed a female Swallowtail dipping down into the Italian parsley and then fluttering about. She was depositing her eggs as she moved from plant to plant. It was a magnificent event to watch. When she flew over the fence I went on a treasure hunt, to see if I could find one of her eggs. I espied a bright yellowish-green sphere-shaped object and assumed that I had found one. Nature protects itself often by camouflaging with its surroundings, and I was lucky to find the one that I did.

We took it home and within days the egg darkened and a teeny, tiny black caterpillar emerged. It was microscopic. For the next little while, it seemed to disappear as it hid among the Italian parsley leaves. I could see its tiny droppings, so I knew it was there. Eventually it was big enough to be seen with the naked eye. It looked as if someone had painted orange and white on its black, canvas body. Some people even describe it as looking like bird droppings. Eventually, the caterpillar transformed into its chrysalis, and it was gifted to a friend's class.

A couple weeks later I received a phone call from Emelie's excited students. They had a Swallowtail butterfly. I was invited to watch the release the next day but unfortunately, the caretaker had accidentally let it out of its container and now it was missing. It was somewhere in the classroom. Eventually, it made an appearance and was released to its new found freedom. Tess, one of Emelie's students wrote me a lovely detailed message about the release, since I was unable to attend. To remember her lovely gesture, I was able to gift her with a Swallowtail ornament.

Patience (Cecropia Moth)

March 23, 2017

I was out walking one day last Fall, and found a huge green caterpillar crossing my path. I took it home and within hours it had tucked itself under a leaf and spun a cocoon. It was donated to my friend Kate's class and now that it is Spring, the class is checking it daily to see signs that it is going to emerge as a large Cecropia moth.

May 1, 2017

I received these texts from Kate today announcing the moth's arrival.

This is our poem today…

"Just when the caterpillar thought its life was over… he began to fly".

This guy hatches to hear it!!! Unbelievable!!!"

Butterflies as Distractions
(Focusing on the Task at Hand)

March 23, 2017

I must admit if there's a butterfly, my attention will be on it. I find them absolutely fascinating to watch!

I once travelled to Uganda, Africa to help build a classroom for AIDS orphans, at the Watoto village. We were moving a pile of bricks from one place to another by forming a human chain and throwing one brick at a time, down the line. It was a very clever, yet primitive way to do it. You would have a brick tossed to you, and you would pass it down the line. Two little white butterflies danced by, and of course, my attention turned to them. Not a good move when you're having bricks tossed to you. Luckily, my reflexes took over and I learned quickly to focus on the task at hand.

Pollinator Gardens Created by Dedicated Volunteers

March 23, 2017

If you plant for them, they will come!

Stratford, Ontario, besides being known for its Shakespearean Festival, is known for its exquisite gardens. Quin Malott, the Parks and Forestry Manager, along with his staff create world class gardens which are admired and appreciated by the many tourists that visit our lovely city.

The Stratford and District Horticultural Society takes on some of the gardens and keeps them looking beautiful.

I was walking through their newest garden on Brittania Circle last Fall, when I saw a single Monarch traveling from flower to flower. He especially enjoyed the Butterfly Bushes (also known as Buddleia), which are at their peak at that time of the year. The butterfly was putting on fat reserves, preparing for its long migratory journey. I couldn't help but think how wonderful it was that the members of this organization offered their time, tools, and expertise to our fine community. There were so many other pollinators in the garden that evening, also sipping on sweet nectar and enjoying the fruits of their labor. This garden not only beautifies our city but provides valuable habitat for these productive insects. As the sun began to set in the sky, the Monarch flew off to find a roosting place for the night. How great it is when man and beast work together in harmony!

With the addition of Milkweed plants, this garden was certified as a Monarch Waystation, ready to serve not only Monarchs but other pollinators as well.

Changing the Way We
Perceive Things

March 27, 2017

I have often said we need to change the name of milkweed to milkflower. That simple, little change could transform the way people think about this necessary and magnificent plant. It has such an incredibly scented flower. Even Monarch flower, would be an appropriate name!

In French, the word for milkweed is "asclepiade" derived from Latin. It is not referred to being a weed at all.

Born in the early 1800's, Ralph Waldo Emerson was quoted as saying, "What is a weed? A plant whose virtues have not yet been discovered."

At one time, not that long ago, milkweed was considered to be a noxious weed in Ontario, Canada. That perception changed when we humans realized that Monarch butterflies were becoming endangered and this was the only food source for their larvae (caterpillars).

I wish a photo could capture its lovely scent.

Joe Pye weed, is also a beautiful plant, attracting all kinds of pollinators. Again, having the word weed in its name can turn a person away from planting it.

We also need to change the way we perceive bees. They are not something we need to fear, if we just leave them alone as they go about their business. They don't call them "busy bees" for nothing. Bees are very necessary for our food production.

One day my class was going on a bus trip and the kids started to scream hysterically. When I asked what the problem was, they informed me that there was a bee flying around the bus. I simply and calmly opened the window and it flew out. It was the perfect time to educate them about the importance of bees in our world, how it's better to remain calm and quiet, and that bees really weren't out to sting them. It is their only form of defense, when in harm's way.

All of us benefit from the service of pollinators. According to the Ministry of Agriculture and Food in Ontario, "Pollination services provide nearly $1 billion in services in Ontario contributing to a sustainable food supply."

Belonging to "W.I.N.G.S"

(Women in Netweaving Groups Soar)

March 27, 2017

When I first retired, I joined W.I.N.G.S. It was a great way to enlarge my circle of friends, which is exactly why the founders of the group, Ev Scott and her lovely daughter Jaimie Martin, had created it.

Whenever I mention going to a W.I.N.G.S. meeting, people assume it has something to do with butterflies. I chuckle! I guess you could say it's a group for women where we come together, because together, we can do more. Each meeting is different, and we learn so much about various interesting topics. We are exposed to new ideas and doors open for us. We mostly laugh but sometimes cry together. We learn and grow, expanding our world experiences. We talk and listen as we learn. We play and work together in perfect harmony. We bring out the best in each other. We celebrate the similarities we share as women, as well as our individualities. We celebrate the gifts of others, and often discover we have gifts we didn't even know we had. We share our gifts and together we SOAR!

Last spring, we filled two tables for a breast-cancer charity fundraiser called "Bras for the Cause." Of course our topic was wings, and of course my bra looked like a butterfly. We had other kinds of wings too! Like Owl wings! It was such a fun gathering of great women supporting a wonderful cause. Even our meeting to prepare for the evening was full of laughs, as we crafted our new bras together.

We were at our Annual Wings Night, and I won the journal that I ended up writing this book in. So I owe it to my wing sister, Dee who provided the door prizes for that evening.

It was some of my W.I.N.G.S. sisters that reminded me that it wasn't crazy that all these Monarch magical moments were happening to me, or that this book was practically writing itself. It was miraculous!

Following the Monarchs

March 27, 2017

Sarah Dykman's journey takes me back to the Fall of 2005, when Vick Gutierrez traveled from Montreal, Canada and followed the five thousand kilometre migration of the Monarchs to the mountains in Mexico, in his ultralight plane. Our family had the pleasure of meeting him along his route at the Greenway Garden Center.

Harrison, my classroom bear was delighted to have a chance to sit in the ultralight. He was reminded of his travels earlier that year to the Monarch mountains, where he became Mariposa Monarca .

Harrison gets a ride in a Ultralight plane that is following the Monarch butterflies to Mexico!

You too can fly with Vick by checking out "Papalotzin the movie, la pelicula" on YouTube.

My Monarch Coin

March 27, 2017

After my wedding rings were stolen, I struggled at the thought of replacing them. My eyes filled with tears every time I entered a jewelry store. I thought perhaps I would tattoo a butterfly on my ring finger. That way no one could take it from me.

The Royal Canadian Mint just happened to come out with a new, three dollar coin. They called it "Celebration of Love". Again, the timing was perfect. It was created by artist, Joel Kimmel. It has two Monarchs looking at each other, which are representing two souls in love, and they are perched on a heart shaped Swarovski crystal. They are surrounded by my favourite butterfly bushes and coneflowers, and there is also an etched Swallowtail butterfly, in the background. Not only was the timing right, it was the perfect gift from Mark.

Honouring Citizen Scientists

March 27, 2017

There are many people looking out for the future of Monarchs, and all pollinators. They work hard and don't get paid a cent, but the rewards are more valuable than gold. Again, working together and doing a little bit, adds up to a lot.

Many people report their Monarch sightings to Monarch Watch. That helps scientists follow and study the migration patterns. There are people like Bruce Parker, who Mark and I had the pleasure of meeting, by chance, when we visited Hawk Cliff. He was netting Monarchs ever so gently, weighing them, tagging them and checking for OE spores. He records his findings, releases the butterflies and reports to Monarch Watch. Bruce, created a wonderful Facebook page entitled, "Monarchs Migrating Through Ontario". Be sure to check it out to see what's happening in the world of Monarchs.

Others raise Monarchs from either the egg or caterpillar stage. This helps protect them from predators until they are adults.

The gardeners help them by planting milkweed and nectar plants, creating Monarch Way Stations. These provide breeding grounds in the summer months, and feeding and resting grounds in the Fall, when it's time for them to migrate. Some gardeners are even converting lawns into gardens specifically designed with pollinators in mind.

Teachers can teach their students, so when they grow up, they can be stewards of the Earth who respect nature. These teachers might be parents of children or people who just want to spread the word. Teachers come in many different forms.

I met a woman who travels to Mexico each year to buy tags that have been found by the locals, in the overwintering grounds. These tags are returned to Monarch Watch so scientists can see how far these marvelous creatures have traveled. Each tag tells an amazing story of where the monarch started and where it ended up. This is such valuable information to collect, and eliminates the guesswork. Who knows? Perhaps they will invent a GPS for Monarchs!

Sharing information on social media can make people aware of what is happening with Monarchs and it is an easy way to be part of the solution. All with a push of a button.

Perhaps I Do See Butterflies Everywhere

March 29, 2017

I had gone into the Emerald Muse store (www.emeraldmuseworks. com) and was drawn to the fluorite crystals for some reason. They come in many different colors, sizes and shapes. I finally settled on one that is blue on one side and the rest looks like frozen ice, and about the size of a walnut shell. Felicitas, the knowledgeable owner said it was known to heighten intuition and look at a situation with less emotion. After struggling for two months with the emotional roller coaster that came with the theft of my jewelry, I felt it would be an excellent rock to place on my jewellery box as a reminder.

The very next morning, I decided to hold it while I did my morning meditation. The sun was streaming through the window revealing a beautiful day outside. I was drawn to take a closer look at the fluorite as the sun shone through it. I gazed into the glassy ocean and was mesmerized at what I saw. I could see a butterfly shape, etched into the stone. Any way I looked at it, I kept seeing a butterfly. I even saw a heart, an angel with tiny butterflies at the base of her skirt and praying hands. As I moved the rock, I could see the butterfly turning into a dragonfly that had a heart in its center. It kept me amused and entertained as I tried to document my findings with my camera. This rock although not very big, surprisingly held a lot within.

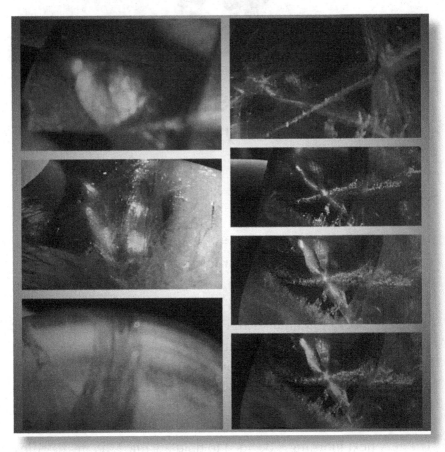

I wasn't sure why I was attracted to fluorite at the time, but many months later I discovered that green fluorite when placed in your garden is known to attract butterflies.

Lately, I've been using the expression, "It's crazy" as the synchronicities continue. "It's miraculous!" is a more positive way of looking at it. As my scientific husband would say, "It's synchronicity with a purpose." I also think it means, "what you look for, is what you will find". That's why it's important to stay positive and choose to look for the good in the world.

The Final Day of Writing
(or so I Thought)

March 31, 2017

My final day of writing! After finishing the first journal I thought I was done…but there was more. Now I have finally run out of butterfly experiences to write about, after exactly two months…. although I'm sure there will be many more, in the days to come.

And I was right!

April 5, 2017

Today, a musical friend who came into the store I was working at, suggested writing a Butterfly Song. I got right to work and this metamorphosed.

Butterfly Heaven

The sun is shining. The butterflies are free.
This must be heaven, all around me.

All of a sudden, the sky turns dark.
The lightning creates a fiery spark.

The butterflies hide as the rain pelts down.
There is no need to wear a frown.

It's through these storms we do grow strong.
Just hold on, it won't be long.

Until darkness turns back to light.
And once again the day is bright.

Raindrops sparkling in the light,
Creating rainbows. Nature's delight.

So open your eyes and see with your mind.
A piece of heaven you will find.

Right here on Earth, yes right here.
We can see heaven. It's crystal clear.

So choose to be happy. Let negativity go.
Just try it out, for it is so.

With a song in your heart and a smile on your face
Look around and truly see this place.

Even when it's raining, beauty is there.
Just dance around without a care.

It's all in the way we look at a thing
And all the challenges that life can bring.

Each day it's what we choose to see
That make up our reality.

What you look for, you will find.
So what kind of life do you have in mind?

Look for the people who go that extra mile
To lift you up and make you smile.

Look for your passion, that gives you zest
And makes your life the very best.

Look above the clouds where the butterflies go.
The sun is always shining beyond them, you know.

My children tell me that life is not all rainbows and butterflies. I tell them life is about enduring the storms to find the rainbows and with time the caterpillars always turn into splendid butterflies, that are free to fly.

A challenge to you! Look for things in the world that give you joy. Take a photo and put it some place to remind you of what makes you happy. What you look for, you will find. I bet you can't take just one!

My kitty, Angel makes me happy!

A Spring Surprise

May 23, 2017

It was a beautiful spring day, so we decided to take my 89 year old mother-in-law to see Webster's Falls. When we arrived, there weren't any parking spots left, so we decided to go to Sherman Falls which was close by. The road into the falls was closed so we had to turn around. We came to a parking lot for the Dundas Conservation Area and decided to explore.

The post said, "The Monarch Trail" and there were some tender milkweed plants all around the trail's entrance. On social media, I had read reports of Monarchs being found in Ontario, so I decided to check the milkweed for eggs, and guess what? Four Monarch eggs were found. I was so excited! Monarch season had started early and I was so happy. I hope this is an indication of the kind of summer we were going to have.

May 11, 2018

It was! The Monarchs came early and stayed late. My kind of summer! Lots of Monarch magic!!

Planting Ted's Garden

June 3, 2017

Today, the Ted Blowes Memorial Pollinator Peace Garden was planted with various types of milkweed and a variety of nectar plants. The weather was beautiful and many people came out to help get the plants into the garden. Everyone worked cooperatively with a smile on their face, and as we know, many hands make light work.

Ethan Elliott, a local high school student, initiated a proposal for Stratford to become a Bee City. On April 10, 2017, Mayor Dan Mathieson signed a resolution for the City of Stratford to accept the designation and commit to the standards of the Bee City Program. Ethan is a member of Nature Ontario and many of the students from this organization came to help. Ted Blowes would have been proud of the youth involved in the planting of this garden.

The Communities in Bloom committee that knew and loved Ted, were there supporting his project as well as many members of the community, both young and old.

When everyone had left, after a productive morning of planting, it was great to see the bee who was enjoying a snack in the new garden. This was just the first of many.

Mama Monarch Was Here!

June 12, 2017

Today my friend, Lorraine and I went to check the Ted Blowes Memorial Pollinator Peace Garden. We were ecstatic to find four Monarch eggs. Lorraine's first ever! Just the beginning of Monarch magic for her! Now to see if they will eclose in time for the opening of the garden!

So it didn't take the Monarchs very long to find the milkweed planted in this public garden! If you plant for them, they will come!

May 23, 2018

The Monarchs emerged too early to keep them until the opening, but another surprise was in store for that special day.

Monarch Magic

June 26, 2017

Today would have been my parents' 74th anniversary. It was also the day of my Aunt Florence's Celebration of Life. She was 98 years old and had survived breast cancer, 49 years ago. I was honoured to be asked to be a pallbearer and read "The Butterfly's Promise" at the graveside.

My first Monarch of the season came out yesterday and it was ready to fly away, today.

After the luncheon, I looked out the door and it was pouring rain. I said, "Boy, do we ever need a miracle if this butterfly is going to be able to be released!" I checked a few minutes later and the rain had halted and the sun was coming out in full force. Wow! It was as if someone had turned off the tap. The dark clouds had been erased! There were a few drops of rain as we drove to the cemetery, fifteen kilometers away.

When we arrived at the gravesite, it hailed! Yes! It hailed! As the hail rolled off of the umbrellas, I lost all hope that the Monarch was going to be released.

After the minister stopped speaking, the sky cleared instantly and the sun came out once again. I couldn't believe it! The timing was impeccable! The Monarch flew beautifully up to the heavens to honour my dear Aunt Florence, as I read "The Butterfly"s Promise". That is Monarch magic at work again!

I very rarely have a Monarch this time of the year. Monarch magic!

When we came home, there were seven more Monarchs that had eclosed and two more ready to come out, the next day.

July 11, 2018

I received this beautiful note from my cousin today.

"Dear Barb,

I'll always be so grateful for your kindness and thoughtfulness in bringing the Monarch to Mom's funeral. Letting me do the release brought such peace. It was also symbolic. When the Monarch soared upwards, I felt it was like Mom's soul soaring to heaven. So beautiful! Love, Cousin Bonnie xxoo"

July 16, 2018

Clearly, I'm afraid to stop writing this book. Am I fearful that the Monarch magic in my life will also stop? Tonight proved to me that it won't.

I was to meet a young family at Ted's garden at 7:00 p.m. to give them a lesson on planting milkweed. They had a patch of land that they wanted to repurpose for pollinators. I had suggested that Ice Ballet milkweed would be a beautiful plant to fill in this space and it was blooming profusely in Ted's garden. They would be able to see how gorgeous and useful this plant is. At 5:30 p.m., it was pouring rain and we thought we would have to postpone our meeting until tomorrow. I suggested that if the Sun happened to appear before seven o'clock we should meet, as their three kids might enjoy releasing the Monarch I had, that was ready to fly free.

Well, the Sun made an appearance and we decided to go ahead with our original plan. When I left home, it was beautiful, but the closer I got to Ted's garden the harder the rain fell. I didn't dare feel sad about it, as the gardens had been crying for rain for a long time. As I sat in the car waiting for the family to arrive, I wondered whether there was about to be some Monarch magic. I sure hoped so.

I saw the kids walking towards the garden in their colourful rain boots, sheltered from the rain under their parents' umbrellas. As I got out of the car to greet them, I was prepared to dance in the rain... but I didn't have to. The rain magically stopped! All I could say was, "Monarch magic!" and "thank you!" Butterflies don't dance in the rain, so I was happy the release could go ahead!

I presented the Ford family with their very own caterpillar and went back to the car to get the Monarch butterfly. They were about to capture Monarch fever. The children buzzed with so many questions about their new friend and decided to call it Robin. I still get as excited as the kids, talking about the amazing metamorphosis that a Monarch goes through in its lifetime. I continue to marvel at children and their curiosity.

We climbed to the top of the bridge to release the butterfly. After a quick lesson on the differences between a male and female Monarch, it was decided that this one was a male. It exhibited the two black dots on its lower wings. It tickled each of the children's noses before flying off to roost in the trees.

As the Monarch basked in the setting sunlight, we went down to the milkweed patch to hunt for Monarch caterpillars and eggs. We found two more caterpillars! Now each child would have their own, thanks to Sam's observant eyes. A newly hatched tiny caterpillar for 3 year old Cullen, a slightly bigger one for 9 year old Olivia and a half grown one for 11 year old Sam. Monarch magic!

Each time I've visited Ted's garden this week, a Monarch has been circling the four wings of the garden. Tonight was no exception! We all just stood there and watched it in awe. I'm sure the butterfly was just as happy as we were, that the Sun had decided to shine upon us this evening. At first we thought it was the butterfly the children had just freed, but it was still resting peacefully on the tree after its first flight.

The Ford family went home to plant for pollinators, beautify their home and embark on an educational and exciting journey. It is always nice to see parents teaching their children how to make this world a better place.

If you plant for pollinators, they will come!...and they do bring a lot of joy with them!

Little Cullen fell asleep as soon as he got back to the car; hanging on to the caterpillars' enclosure. Butterfly dreams!

Allan's Wings

June 27, 2017

This morning, Lisa and her children, Liam and Noelle met at the airport to do a butterfly release for Lisa's loving husband, Allan. His life had been taken weeks earlier, on June 2, 2017, doing what he loved. Flying! The sky was blue with white fluffy clouds but it felt like it was going to rain. It was only 10 degrees C. (50 degrees F.) so the butterflies couldn't fly. We took a few pictures, until the clouds turned dark, the wind picked up and rain began to fall. Slowly at first, and then the clouds burst open like a water balloon. As the rain washed away our tears, we realized the release wasn't going to happen...at least not then.

The weather report said it would be sunny and warm by 2:00 p.m. The butterflies were meant to be with them a little while longer. We decided to call it a morning and wait until the weather improved. Noelle had to go off to work. Lisa and Liam released theirs as soon as the sun came out. As they did, a plane flew over them. It made them smile, for it was the thing Allan loved most, next to his family.

That evening, there was a second attempt at a release, this time with more family and friends. The sun cooperated and created a beautiful summer evening, perfect for sending butterflies up into the heavens. A perfect release for a man who loved flying. As the Monarchs flew upwards, many of the tears turned into smiles. Allan would have been smiling too, seeing the love and support being received at this time.

It seems that the Monarchs help connect heaven and earth.

It was amazing that the Monarchs arrived early this year to make this possible.

A few weeks later, Liam had a Monarch fly right into his truck window for a wee visit and then it was off! Perhaps it was one of the ones released in memory of his Dad???

May 9, 2018

Lisa continues to live life with a smile on her face. She has got to be one of the most inspiring, courageous and amazing women I know. Lisa had also lost both of her parents in the eight months prior to Allan leaving this world; her Dad just the month before. Her house was undergoing major renovations, but she persevered. On Allan's 49th birthday, she threw a party complete with balloons, cake and Allan's favourite foods. Allan must be so proud of her! I know everyone who knows her, is.

May 28, 2018

Lisa never ceases to amaze me! The first anniversary of Allan's parting is approaching and she has asked people to post their best memory of Allan. What a wonderful way for her and the kids to turn a very difficult time into a time of remembrance and reflection.

June 26, 2018

Today, Lisa and her young neighbour, Kelly released this season's very first Monarch in Allan's memory. I am not surprised that moments before the release there was a cloud shaped like an airplane in the sky.

Lisa certainly has risen above these challenges and transformed into an even stronger, brighter version of herself. She never fails to encourage others to appreciate and love the people in their lives. Life is short and every time we say goodbye, it could be the last time.

A Butterfly for Julia

July 7, 2017

The first time I saw Julia was Halloween, and she was parading through the school I taught at, dressed as a beautiful angel. You couldn't help but notice her with her sparkling halo and white, flowing gown. The following year, I had the pleasure of having Julia in my grade two class.

Julia was a special student for many reasons. Her gentle kindness was appreciated by all and she always wore a smile. Even when she had to leave the room daily to work with a respiratory therapist or take enzymes to help her digest her food. Julia was born with Cystic Fibrosis and never complained.

She had an unusually mature presence and she was wise beyond her years. Julia's family was always there to support her and maintained a positive attitude. I used to pass their home each morning as I walked to school and send them warm thoughts. I marvelled at how they demonstrated gratitude and saw things with humour.

When Julia was 15, her lungs were deteriorating and she endured a double lung transplant. At the time, (1998) she was the youngest person to receive this surgery. She was able to breathe once again and had the chance to visit the Notre Dame Cathedral in Paris, France. She was proud of herself for making it up the many stairs to the top; something she would never have been able to do before her surgery. She was also able to blow out her birthday candles that year. Something we take for granted.

Once again, Julia needed and received another double lung transplant. When you hugged her, you couldn't help but think of the wonderful gift a donor family gave to this family. Not once, but twice.

Julia's sister, Emily, tells how important organ donation is when it comes to saving lives. Her sister lived for over a decade more and was given the chance to grow into a woman, fall in love and create so many wonderful memories with her family.

In 2011, Julia left behind all the people who loved her. Her ashes were spread from a helicopter over the Haleakala Crater in Hawaii, one of the most beautiful places in the world. Very fitting for one of the most beautiful souls who ever walked this earth. Above the clouds, where the sun is always shining and below the stars which shine on her every night.

Her Mother, Gail, released some Monarchs today, not only for our precious Julia, but for the medical team that made the best life possible for her. She also released Monarchs in memory of others who fought Cystic Fibrosis along with Julia. Gail is always looking out for others and faces each day with a sense of humour. She is so full of gratitude for life and you can't help but admire the strong woman she is.

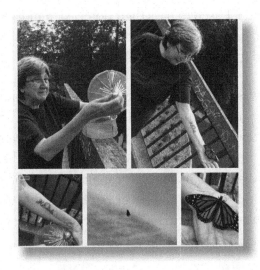

Another Dragonfly Visits

July 8, 2017

I was out in our pollinator garden admiring the colourful blooms and the many visitors. All of a sudden there was this very friendly dragonfly. It jumped from the flower to my finger. It wasn't even afraid of our cat, Angel. I'm beginning to think they are quite tame beings or are just jealous of the attention I give to the Monarchs.

How I love our pollinator garden! It makes me stop, breathe and smell the roses! I love watching a butterfly drink the sweet nectar with its straw-like proboscis.

The Day Before Ted's
Garden Opening

July 19, 2017

Today I had another unusual visitor. The plants that were going to be planted at the opening of Ted's garden were sitting on my driveway, ready to be transported the next day. A very tattered Monarch flew to the flowers and quite enjoyed their sweet nectar. It lingered for a long time and I just enjoyed its presence.

I couldn't help but wonder what it had endured in its lifetime. Its wings were thin and weak; very similar to the Monarchs that had migrated to Mexico and had spent the winter huddled together in the trees. It was very friendly and even walked onto my hand. What was it trying to tell me? Did Ted have something to do with this special moment in time?

The Grand Opening of the Ted Blowes Memorial Pollinator Peace Garden

July 20, 2017

The day before the grand opening of the garden, I had been with the Communities in Bloom judges all day photographing their visit to our beautiful city. To my surprise, I had six Swallowtail butterflies out of their chrysalids when I arrived home. Their wings would be dry just in time for the grand opening of the garden. How perfectly timed!

In the past, I only had Swallowtails in the Fall in my classroom. They would enter their chrysalis and hide until spring. These butterflies were once caterpillars ravishly eating my friend Sheila's, dill plants. She had called me and asked if I would come and rescue them from her dill.

The evening before, the weatherman was calling for rain and my Communities in Bloom fellow committee members were bringing this to my attention. With no alternate plans, we needed some Monarch magic. You can't have a garden dedication indoors and with family coming from a great distance, it just had to happen, rain or shine. Sometimes you just need to let go and trust that things will work out for the best…and they did!

As I drove to the garden the next morning, raindrops fell on my windshield like tears from heaven. Just a lovely gentle rain! I'm sure the plants in the pollinator garden loved the cool morning beverage.

When I arrived at the park, the rain stopped and we started to set up for the dedication.

We no sooner finished, when suddenly the sky let loose once more. Luckily, we were armed with many umbrellas. I thought of our planned butterfly release. The butterflies would never be able to fly in this rain! Again, luck was on our side and the rain only lasted for a few minutes and the guests began to arrive.

Just when we were about to start, the sky darkened once more, but this time the sun took pity on us and peeked out from behind the clouds, ready to shine for the rest of the day. The temperature was perfect and the garden ceremony began.

The butterflies were released throughout the ceremony. They quickly landed on the garden flowers to sip the rich nectar. It was a delight to see and they certainly entertained the many guests. They were a wonderful addition to the agenda and demonstrated what the garden was all about, providing nutrition and habitat for pollinators!

Mayor Dan Mathieson and John Nater, our Member of Parliament had fun releasing their butterflies. One even ended up on the Mayor's nose.

Photo credit: Fred Gonder

Courtney and Meredith Pearce, two beautiful ballerinas, looked like gorgeous flowers as they danced to the "Butterfly Waltz" throughout the garden and ended their performance by releasing two sweet Swallowtails. They represented the younger generation who will grow up, and hopefully see pollinators with their children. As Audrey Hepburn said, "To plant a garden, is to believe in tomorrow."

Photo Credit: Fred Gonder

The garden stone and the educational sign were unveiled and the formalities ended with "O Canada" and a butterfly release with Ted's family, in memory of their loved one, who they shared with our community and the rest of the world.

Everything turned out beautifully!

Photo credit: Brilliant Images, Stratford

After the Opening of Ted's Garden

July 21, 2017

This appeared as a Facebook memory. Need I say anything more?

May 25, 2018

This morning I woke up and I asked Ted for a sign that he was still here. Around 11:00 a.m., I created a copy of my book and the first page was on my laptop screen. Suddenly, my cat, Shadow went scampering across the keyboard. I must admit I wasn't too happy with her. When I looked at the new letters she was responsible for, I saw "gttb". I'm not sure what the "gt" stood for but I'm sure the "tb" stood for Ted Blowes. You just can't make this stuff up.

Ryder's First Butterfly Release

July 25, 2017

After rescuing my friend Sheila's dill plants, I was rewarded with beautiful Swallowtail butterflies for the opening of the Ted Blowes Memorial Pollinator Peace Garden. Five days later, a late bloomer arrived. I think it was waiting for Sheila's young son to experience his first butterfly release. It did my heart good watching Sheila share the beauty of nature with Ryder, at such a tender young age of one. It happened quickly and the butterfly flew off in the direction of the dill plants from where it began!

A Great Gathering of
Butterfly Enthusiasts

August 14, 2017

Today, Mark and I went to Greenway Garden Center to hear Sara Dykman's presentation of her Butterbike Journey, from Mexico up into Canada. I hadn't seen her since she started her journey, at the beginning of March, in Mexico. It was awesome to see her again and introduce her to Mark. Mariposita was still fastened under her bike seat, just a little dirtier, accompanying her every move.

It was a great gathering of butterfly enthusiasts including John G. Powers, Donald Davis and Kimberly Parry, The Butterfly Whisperer ®. I was thankful that Sara was able to change her original proposed route to make this happen.

It was a pleasure to meet Jeff Grant, a young lad who was just bursting with excitement for butterflies. He taught us so much as he showed us around Greenway's gorgeous pollinator garden with great enthusiasm. Perhaps he will be a famous lepidopterist one day. (That is a person who studies or collects moths and butterflies.) He is well on his way, with the specimens that John Powers gifted him with that day.

Mark was able to get some incredible photos in the garden, especially this one of the Monarch and the Hummingbird Moth on the Buddleia.

We visited the greenhouse to see the butterflies and I had the pleasure of chatting with The Butterfly Whisperer® who has been raising Monarchs for over forty years. As her name suggests, she whispers to each butterfly a loving message to carry, as they are being released. That's just one piece of her fascinating butterfly-led life.

Kim shared with me her vivid memory of the first time she saw a Monarch emerge from its chrysalis. She was only five years old, yet knew she had just witnessed a miracle. It was so impactful that it continues to influence every aspect of her life. When our conversation moved from our butterfly passion to our careers, it didn't surprise me to learn that she uses the butterfly life-cycle as the foundation of her Transformational Coaching practice. She explained that many people spend their lives acting like caterpillars even though we've been gifted with the human equivalent of wings. Kim encourages everyone to go out and share their wings with the world.

Kim always looks forward to the summer months when she is able to share her live butterflies with others, whether it's through educational presentations, group releases, or intimate, customized butterfly experiences at her Monarch Motel™(backyard greenhouse).

Through her special work with grieving children, as well as women healing from abuse, Kim has become known for 'giving wings to silent voices'. To better share her butterfly gift on a global scale, she has also made available a truly one-of-a-kind service. People from around the world send their personal messages to the The Butterfly Whisperer®. She whispers these heartfelt messages to her beloved Monarch Messengers™ on their behalf, including messages to loved ones that have passed on. That just warms my heart!

It didn't take long for me to understand how Kim ended up with the nickname, "Sunshine". She and I hit it off immediately and we had a lot in common. We even discovered that both of us got married at 11:11 a.m.! When I returned home, I realized that we were already friends on Facebook. I wasn't surprised! (You too can connect with her on Facebook at www.facebook.com/TheButterflyWhisperer, and learn more about her inspirational work via her website at www. TheButterflyWhisperer.com) I find it interesting that Kim whispers to Monarchs and Monarchs whisper to me, thus the title of my book, "When a Butterfly Speaks...Life Lessons Among Its Whispers".

That evening I heard the news that a former student's dog had passed away. I had a Monarch come out that day so, in the morning I took the butterfly to the three children, who were very sad about their dear pet. They became butterfly whisperers that day, as they whispered their heartfelt messages for their beloved dog, to that Monarch.

"You were the very best dog ever!"

"I will miss you. I hope you are having fun up there!"

"I love you!"

The butterfly was to deliver their messages to dog heaven...but paused in the garden for awhile before taking off into the blue sky. It was so touching.

Sara Dykman Visits Stratford

August 15-18, 2017

Sara Dykman arrived at our house on her trusted bike. The next few days were extremely busy as we packed as much as we could into this short visit. Her schedule in Ontario, exploring the Canadian end of the migration, was intense. She made numerous presentations, educating people about Monarchs, and motivating them to help by planting milkweed, the only food source for their caterpillars. We visited local pollinator gardens and many people had the chance to see Sara's bike, and hear of her adventures. Sara even had the chance to visit the beach in Goderich for a day. It was a time to hike, relax, eat ice cream cones and capture memories with our cameras. Butterfly waffles were on the menu for breakfast each day.

Before we could blink, it was time for Sara to ride on to London, Point Pelee and Lakeshore for further presentations. Then she would leave Canada, following the Monarchs back to Mexico through the United States. To celebrate Sara completing the first half of her journey, we released a Monarch who would soon be on it way to Mexico too. The race was on! Who would get to Mexico first?

Butterfly Birthday

August 6, 2017

Eight newly eclosed Monarchs, plus an eighth birthday to celebrate, equals Serenity's birthday surprise.

What can be better than beginning a celebration with the release of eight Monarch butterflies? Releasing them one at a time!

It was a beautiful summer day and the Monarchs were ready to go. Serenity savoured each release and enjoyed every moment. The smile on her face said it all. Seeing the joy and wonder as a child frees a butterfly, reminds me of the importance of protecting all creatures so these children have the chance to share these magnificent insects with their children.

The next stop was a ditch with milkweed. Exploring and looking for Monarch treasures was very successful. We were excited to find some Monarch eggs.

Then we were off to the country ice cream shop, The Organic Oasis to have a treat. A Wood Nymph butterfly flew in to join the celebration as we enjoyed the enchanting picnic area.

A rock pile can be so much fun, especially when your rock splits into four pieces and creates a butterfly. Does this sound familiar?

Sometimes the best things in life are the simple things!

Speaking of birthdays, I had found a birthday gift left at my door. It was the most beautiful bamboo basket, so perfect for butterfly releases. My orange chiffon containers had seen better days, so this was a very special well-timed gift from a lovely friend who remembered my butterfly passion. Thanks, Sue! The only problem was, it was November and I would have to wait until the summer to use it!

July, 2018

Sue's gift has been incorporated into some very beautiful moments. They have been well worth waiting for!

This evening was enchanting! My friend, Lesley had lost her dear Mother, last summer. In order to celebrate her birthday and her life, a beautiful Monarch emerged, specifically to do just that. We met at Ted's garden and were amazed how the butterfly flew up to the treetops. Usually a butterfly released in the evening is eager to roost, but not tonight. This lovely lady butterfly danced ever so gracefully among the emerald branches, glowing in the setting evening sunlight. We just watched in awe. Circling! Spiraling! Twirling! Nature's ballet at its best! Lesley, being a dancer, could feel the joy in this release and the dance of freedom. Her Mother was now free to fly, after devoting much of her life, caring for and protecting her physically disabled son.

You are Never Too Old to Experience New Things

August 20, 2017

Four Monarchs eclosed today! As their wings dried to prepare for their first flight, I wondered who would be the recipients?? I've never had so many Monarchs! This summer has been exceptional! They arrived early and we were finding eggs and caterpillars left, right and center. Perhaps taking milkweed off the noxious weed list and creating pesticide-free habitats was working. I've been surprised how every butterfly has had a person who needed to be a part of its release, for many different reasons.

The next thing I knew, I was driving to Cambridge to visit my Mom's best friend, Laura who was days away from turning 100 years young. Now that doesn't come along every day! She was like a second mother to me when I was growing up and helped me celebrate many of my birthdays, always with one of her exquisitely decorated cakes. What fun it was to see her delight when releasing a butterfly for each quarter century of her life.

You are never too old to experience new things. We also took her cotton candy. Another first!...and it was wonderful to watch as a spectator.

Be Careful What You Wish For

August 20, 2017

After experiencing the beautiful dove release at Rachel and Jeff's wedding, I couldn't help but fall in love with Lisa Jensen's doves. So graceful and snowy white!

On Mother's Day, Rachel and I had traveled back to Lisa's delightful bird sanctuary in the Niagara area for a dove release in memory of my dear Mom. It was a lovely afternoon complete with tea, dainties and a true celebration of mothers. The doves flying against the gorgeous blue sky dotted with feathery clouds, was a sight to behold.

Throughout the summer, I have loved engaging in many butterfly releases. I must admit though, that I envy Lisa and her doves. When they are released, they fly back to her home, whereas my Monarchs are gone, never to be seen again. The doves also fly all year around. I have considered getting a pair of doves, but knowing our two cats, Shadow and Angel, they wouldn't approve.

Well today, when I drove my mother-in-law home, a teenager was sitting outside her 18 storey condo with a dove. It had been hanging around the doorway and although looking healthy, was not attempting to fly away. I happened to have my Monarch enclosure in the car, so it was decided that I would take the dove home, away from the busy road nearby. Tomorrow, I will see how it's doing and hopefully release it into the air, where a bird should be.

Barbara J. Hacking

August 21,2017

Morning : The dove is still living in my butterfly cage. We are not sure if it can fly.

Afternoon: After many calls to various agencies I found a vet who rehabilitates wild birds. She was only an hour away and very close to where the dove had been found. It was sad to say goodbye but our cats will be happy.

Butterfly Blessings

August 22, 2017

After many years with very few Monarchs, this summer has truly been uplifting and I am hopeful that the Monarchs are making a comeback.

There are so many things to celebrate in this world. When you just happen to have Monarchs to release to add to the occasion, it puts smiles on the participants' faces.

When celebrating the life of a loved one, I often wonder if these people will ever smile again, especially after a tragic death. It warms my heart when seeing their tears change to ones of joy and remembrance.

During this summer, I was gifted with many Monarchs and miraculously they just happened to make it into many celebratory moments, each unique in their own way. The butterflies would appear in the morning, and before the day was over they would be in the hands of those who needed them. It has been a very magical summer so far, indeed! I have been honoured and humbled to be able to share these special and often private moments.

This morning Katarina, posted a photo on Facebook of her husband, Frank and their daughter, Jensen frolicing in their pool. Chills ran through my body as this special father-daughter moment may not have happened without Frank's kidney transplant, eight months earlier. What made it even more remarkable was that Katarina was the life-giving donor. She was the perfect match and was able to give her husband this treasured gift, that no amount of money could buy.

Six newly-eclosed Monarchs greeted me that morning and were offered to this family, to celebrate the transformation that this magnificent gift gave, not only to Frank, but to all of them.

Frank's transplant was certainly something to celebrate. He had a new lease on life and they were now free to fly into the future and create many more wonderful memories as a family. Frank would be there to see his daughter grow up.

It was a miracle that came about by the grace of our creator, Katarina's selflessness and love, the wondrous medical team's skill and knowledge, the help and support of many friends and family, and Jensen's courage to have both parents in the hospital at the same time. It was Jensen that gave both Frank and Katarina the strength and courage to fight for life during their transplant journey. The day her parents were released from the hospital, Jensen planted three of Canada's 150th tulip bulbs, representing her family. Over the winter, the bulbs would remain buried, covered in snow as they healed. When the tulips burst open in the spring looking like Canadian flags, it would be time again to celebrate not only Canada's 150th birthday, but their restored health. Just like a chrysalis, silent and still, waiting to complete the full metamorphosis into a butterfly, free to fly. Time can heal and transform many things.

As Katarina released a butterfly, she recited a saying that had helped her through tough times, "If your wings are broken, please take mine, so your wings can open too". Frank is now able to fly!

Once again I was amazed at how these butterflies found their way into the perfect hands.

Tonight I was sitting watching TV in the family room, when a moth flew to my hand and tried to nectar on it. Perhaps it was enjoying a salty snack. It stayed for quite awhile and I wondered how it had found its way into our house. I think it must have been the strange-looking caterpillar that I had, that escaped. It was long and skinny and I put it into the Monarch home, curious to see what its adult form would be, and it disappeared. I'm sure it was telling me it metamorphosed without my help. Nature is clever and knows what it is doing.

My, how I love this season and all it has to offer!

August 23, 2017

It must be peak Monarch season as many butterflies were being watched by our cats, Angel and Shadow this morning. I think they enjoy the butterflies as much as Mark and I do. Often we catch them watching "Butterfly TV" as we call it. We find it just as fascinating to watch them.

Today was another special day for Katarina and her mother. They were preparing to celebrate 50 years in Canada. Katherine and her husband, John had immigrated from Sweden when Katarina was just a baby during Canada's 100th year of Confederation. Little did they realize then, that they were importing a very valuable item; Katarina's kidney, so precious and rare. It gets one thinking about how one moment in time, or an action can change the whole course of one's life. It's really mind-boggling to think in such a way. A decision or choice today can set your life in a totally different direction.

I wonder what would have happened if Mark and I had never met. Would I still be as connected to butterflies as I am? Would I be writing this journal? Who knows? It's one of life's little mysteries! Just like the many mysteries of the Monarchs; it's what makes them intriguing.

Another butterfly release was in order today for Katarina and her Mom. It's not every day one can celebrate 50 years of coming to Canada. Just think how that changed history for Katarina, her parents, Jensen and most of all, for Frank !! Katarina released a butterfly for her late father. As it flew upwards, it looked like it was flying up to a cloud, shaped like an angel. This is not the first time I have witnessed this.

Four Butterflies! Four Butterfly Tattoos!

August 24, 2017

Four butterfly tattoos!
Each butterfly representing a very significant time in Andrea Eygenraam's life.
Each butterfly representing the darkness transforming into light.
Each butterfly representing the learning that came with each struggle.
Each butterfly representing the transformation Andrea completed to make her the wonderful person she is today. From being grounded like a caterpillar, to being free to fly through life with a smile on her face.

Three of Andrea's butterfly tattoos contain a semicolon making up the body of the butterfly. In the year 2013, social media began a movement called Project Semicolon. It's purpose was to send hope and love to those battling depression, suicide, addiction and self-injury. Why a semicolon, you may ask? A semicolon is used when the writer could have paused but decided not to. It is a reminder of a person's struggle and victory. They have chosen to live on, despite their darkness.

Andrea's middle tattoo is a tribute to a friend of hers who lost her battle with cancer. Sometimes, the right person comes along, at the right time, with the right words. Andrea's friend, did just that! She showed Andrea unconditional love at the time Andrea was in her chrysalis, transforming from a drug addict back to the land of the living. As Andrea's health and life improved, her friend got sicker and was gone. They say it's not how long we've known someone, but the impact they have made on our life that makes them special.

I first met Andrea at a W.I.N.G.S. meeting back in January. It was her first visit and I was impressed at how after being coerced, by a friend to get up and tell her story, she did. And what a story it was! I was moved by her honesty and her willingness to share such a personal story with complete strangers. I marveled at the fact that she was able to completely change her life around. After coming through a difficult childhood, a toxic, abusive relationship and being addicted to crystal meth, she recovered. She relocated often, trying to find herself, until finally realizing what she needed was inside of herself, all along.

Andrea was about to celebrate ten years of being "clean". That is certainly something to celebrate, and celebrate we did with four beautiful Monarchs on a changeable summer day! At first, it was cool and cloudy and we thought we might have to postpone the release. Monarchs need a wing temperature of 13 degrees C.(55 degrees F.) before they can fly. As soon as the release began, the sun came out only to hide once again, when all the butterflies were freed. Monarch magic at work, I think.

Andrea has made many marvelous changes in her life and is filled with gratitude and appreciation. She now helps others by sharing her story, acting as a certified life coach, and is a published author. (Myinspiredcommunications.com)

A Release For the Hospice

September 7, 2017

This has turned out to be an incredible summer for Monarchs! They arrived early and it's been a pleasure to see so many. I wasn't able to get 100 Monarchs for the hospice fundraiser, but had about twenty ready to go for today's photo shoot, at the lot where the new hospice will be constructed.

The weather had been cool all day but it was supposed to be warm enough by 5:00 p.m., according to the hour by hour weather report. The sun was out and the Monarchs, although slow, did manage to fly upwards over the grounds. Monarch magic!

A Monarch in Maine

October 7, 2017

It was a perfect sunny, Autumn day when we arrived in Cape Elizabeth, ME. We were anxious to explore along the ocean trail as we got off the tourist-carrying trolley and breathed in the fresh, salty air.

The first thing we noticed was the American flag at half mast for the 58 people who died in the Las Vegas shooting, on October 1. A gunman had opened fired on a crowd of people attending the Harvest Music Festival and over 800 people were injured as well. It was a tragedy that was felt greatly by the rest of the world. It dampened our spirits as we were reminded of the events from the previous week.

We then saw a Painted Lady butterfly, nectaring on some dandelions that were blooming for the second time that year. Butterflies have a way of cheering me up and this was perfectly timed.

When dandelions are not sprayed they serve as rich nectar plants for pollinators, early in the Spring and later in the Fall when other plants have died. Humans work hard to get rid of them, although they are valuable plants in many ways. It all boils down to whether you see the dandelion as a weed or a wish. Dandelion greens are high in fibre and contain many important nutrients. This year I decided to pick the unsprayed leaves from our lawn when they were young and tender, and created salads with them. Delicious! No wonder they are becoming a delicacy at many grocery stores. They work well in smoothies, as well. I left the blooms for the many pollinators that needed that early food.

I often have Monarchs show up when I'm feeling sad and I was not disappointed. There, also nectaring on some dandelions was a single female Monarch. We only saw one, but that's all I needed. She would be on her way to Mexico, along the East coast, and she was sipping on liquid gold that would give her the energy to make the long migration. She still had 2,938 miles (or 4,828 km) to get to the magical Monarch mountains, in the States of Mexico and Michoacan. She was so focused on filling her belly that she didn't mind me picking her up, along with the dandelion she was nectaring on. We released her and remembered all those who died or were injured many miles away on that devastating day.

Remembering Sydney...
Sydney's Tenth Birthday

October 19, 2017

From time to time we are touched by people who shine even in the face of grief. The Evan's family does exactly that! They are incredibly inspirational, as they remember their beautiful daughter, Sydney, who passed away shortly after her second birthday, from SIDS.

Today would have been Sydney's tenth birthday! The Evan's family created a Random Act of Kindness Day to celebrate her sweet life. They printed 1500 cards to go with each act of kindness and hoped that people would make this world a better place, as they remembered Sydney. People found many creative ways to make this day one to remember. For examples of what happened that day, you can go to their Facebook Page. (Random Acts of Kindness in Memory of Sydney) or (@RAOK4Syd) or (#RAOK4Syd). Perhaps their story will inspire you to do a random act of kindness. It doesn't have to cost any money. Something as simple as a handwritten note can make someone's day...and I bet it will make your day too!

Today was a glorious, Autumn day complete with sunshine and butterflies. Yes, butterflies! Normally, at this time of the year, the Monarchs are long gone on their journey to Mexico. The chances of finding one on this day would be slim to none, at least here in Stratford, Ontario, Canada. That's why Sydney's family had a butterfly release to celebrate Sydney's 10th birthday back in early July. I had promised Eric, Sydney's brother, a butterfly last spring if

I was fortunate enough to have one, in the Summer. Monarchs have not been plentiful in recent years, so the promise had to come with that condition. Luckily, on the day of their release there were four, one for each of Sydney's parents, Michelle and Duane and one each for Eric and Aubrey. You can see a video of this uplifting release on their Facebook page as well.

This morning I was walking through the gorgeous Shakespearean Gardens and couldn't believe my eyes. There was a Monarch. Only one! She should have been long gone, but no, she was here enjoying the late blooming, nectar flowers. In fact, she was so busy sipping the sweet liquid she didn't notice me watching her. She allowed me to gently pick her up, when she was done. I gave her a wee butterfly kiss, for Sydney, and sent her off on her way. She needed to get going before the cold weather found us. This will probably be the last one seen in this garden this year.

Later, when I returned home, I was greeted by one of these random acts of kindness and was elated. A former student's Mom, Jill, had made beautiful Monarch butterfly cookies. She packaged and distributed them in remembrance of Sydney. Wow! Being one of the many recipients of this kindness, I can tell you "Sydney's Day" was extremely successful, sharing what the world truly needs more of...kindness.

An Interesting Visitor

November 14, 2017

Today would have been my Dad's 103rd birthday. It was about 5 degrees C. (41 degrees F.), and a lovely sunny day. Since it was warm for this time of the year and I felt like celebrating my Dad's birthday, I decorated the front door for Christmas. I know it was a bit early but it was better than waiting until the cold weather set in. After supper, a friend and I were having a meeting. While we were sitting at the kitchen table, a moth kept tapping at the kitchen window. It really was trying hard to get our attention, and it was successful. It persisted knocking at the window which is so unusual, especially at this time of the year. It should have been tucked in somewhere for the winter. I called upstairs to Mark and he went out on the deck to photograph it. Even Mark's presence didn't scare it away. I took pictures from the inside. It was very strange but a beautiful reminder of my dear father's birthday!

Looking out the window at this special visitor

Gratitude

March 6, 2018

Rachel and I have just returned from the magical Monarch mountains. What a busy, stress-free week frolicing with the butterflies. We visited four Monarch sanctuaries and we saw lots of activity when the sun was shining, and lots of clusters when the clouds prevailed. What a treat it was when the kaleidoscope burst into explosions of dancing Monarchs. We met many amazing people who shared these wonderful mountains with us. It was especially wonderful to share the beginning of our adventure with Kelley and Daniel, also from Stratford. By coincidence, we arrived in Macheros the same day.

It was awesome visiting with Sara Dykman once again and hearing about her successful journey. Her Butterbike Project had her following the migratory path of the Monarchs. Nine and a half months and almost 16,500 kilometres later (exactly 10,201 miles), her journey is over, but not her adventures! Time will tell where her life will take her.

After raising Monarchs as a child, it was great for Rachel to finally visit the overwintering grounds. It was awesome to see the transformation from being a busy nurse, to someone who was relaxed and at peace with the world. The awe in her eyes and the smile on her face said it all. She loves this place as much as I do. It truly feels like heaven on earth.

I am not surprised that the video I posted of the millions of Monarchs flying in the sun received over 750,000 views and 4,000 likes, loves or wows in the first week home on Facebook. The world needs to experience the peace, joy and calm that watching the Monarchs in their glory, can bring.

Yesterday, I watched an online class by Robin Sharma where he suggested gratitude journaling for twenty minutes per day. It serves to release emotions and discover the blessings in your life.

Here is my gratitude journaling after visiting the Monarchs in their winter home.

I am grateful for Macheros, the little village beside Cerro Pelon, where many of the Monarchs stay during our winter, and for its glorious sunsets.

I am grateful for the people of Macheros who live a simple, uncomplicated life. Their smiles radiate joy. Their bellies are filled with glorious food from their fields and streams.

I am grateful for the people who guide the horses up the steep mountains so people can experience this beautiful phenomenon, as well as the rangers who protect the butterflies.

I am grateful for Joel and Ellen who had the foresight to create "JM Butterfly Bed and Breakfast" so that people can experience their heavenly home.

I am grateful for Joel's mother (Mama Rosa) and his sisters who masterpieced our amazing, authentic Mexican cuisine. Their guacamole is exquisite! My mouth waters just thinking about it!

I am grateful for the chance to visit with our Monarchs that eclosed here in Canada, late last summer, and migrated many thousands of miles/kilometers to their winter home.

I am grateful for the many wonderful people we met when exploring the Monarch sanctuaries together.

I am grateful that Sara Dykman was able to complete her journey of a lifetime safely and I was able to see her once again.

I am grateful for the chance to visit the elementary school and see a Monarch sitting on a plant in their classroom. It had just emerged. Their playground had milkweed with caterpillars, in their school garden. The chrysalids were all over the playground and untouched by the young students. Respect for their beloved Monarch was evident.

I am grateful for the time I got to spend with my lovely daughter. It was great to share the magic of the Monarch mountains with her.

Both Sides of the Coin

March 18, 2018

I've been home from Mexico for almost two weeks and have been truly amazed at how quickly my video of "El Rosario's meadow of millions of Monarchs" has traveled. 750,000 views! Wow! The power of social media! We don't even need to travel to see the marvels of this wonderful planet. You can see this video on my Facebook page, "When a Butterfly Speaks...Whispered Life Lessons".

I loved reading the comments of how people felt like they were actually witnessing the overwintering grounds, firsthand. Many longed to put it on their bucket list. For others, it conjured up many beautiful memories, and the urgent need to protect the Monarchs.

On the other hand, I was shocked with the comments saying that this would be their worst nightmare.

The butterfly video explosion, reminded me that we all don't see things in the same way and we must respect different viewpoints, to live peacefully. Afterall, the world would be a very dull place without the uniqueness of each individual.

Patience

March 23, 2018

Today, I was listening to Mindvalley Academy's Masterclass, by Srikumar Rao, and he mentioned a poem written in the 1300's, by Rumi. His ancient words hold just as true today, if not more so.

"When I run after what I think I want, my days are a furnace of distress and anxiety. If I sit in my own place of patience, what I need flows to me and without any pain. From this, I understand what I want, also wants me, is looking for me and attracting me. There is a great secret in this for anyone who can grasp it."

It reminds me of a popular butterfly poem by Nathaniel Hawthorne who lived in the 1800's.

"Happiness is like a butterfly, which when pursued is always just beyond your grasp, but which, if you will sit down quietly, may alight upon you."

May 14, 2018

Mark and I were hiking today, enjoying a perfect Spring day in the forest. We were surrounded by tiny blue and white butterflies as we walked the trails. It was very difficult to capture them with our cameras, as they moved so quickly. I saw four resting in one spot so I remembered Hawthorne's poem and sat down. That's when one of the butterflies cautiously explored my hand.

In a fast paced world, where everything is so instant, I think these poems remind us that we need to slow down from time to time, allowing ourselves to breathe deeply and think clearly. Meditation is a good example of putting that into practice. There are many different ways to meditate. The key is finding the one that resonates with you.

Yoga, also an excellent activity with many benefits, teaches one to breathe.

Forest bathing (No! You don't have to take your clothes off for this activity!), which originated in Japan, has also been shown to have many health benefits. Taking in all the gifts nature has to offer, as you walk among the trees, has become a favourite past time for Mark and I. Each adventure is unique and special. Anything that takes us off that treadmill of life, can be beneficial for stress and anxiety levels. Watching butterflies is one of my favourite ways to just slow down and breathe.

My Ticket to Mexico

March 26, 2018

A few days ago, I happened to come across a scrapbook, that I had created. It was my ticket to travel with other Canadian and American teachers to Mexico, to visit the Monarch's overwintering grounds, for the first time. It was entitled "My Butterfly Journey". It was created before the internet and digital cameras. Looking at it truly took me back in time (2005), and I realized how much the world had changed in such a short period of time. I also realized that many of the stories written in this book were written before, in the scrapbook. I believe they would have continued to circulate within me, until I wrote them down and until I was ready to share them with the world.

As Stephen King once said, "Sometimes stories cry out to be told in such loud voices that you write them just to shut them up."

I have now shared them with the world. I can't help but wonder if people will believe these experiences really happened, or think that I am going crazy. Perhaps I should/could have written a fiction story... but then...the stories probably wouldn't have been much different.

March 29, 2018

I woke up early this morning thinking about the title of my book. I needed to shorten the second part. So..."When a Butterfly Speaks... Whispered Life Lessons".

The poem I found in my scrapbook, called, " I Heard a Butterfly Call My Name" inspired me to change it.

I Heard a Butterfly Call My Name

August 26, 2002

I heard a butterfly call my name,
Although he made no sound.
The words that he then shared with me
Were really quite profound.

I heard his message clearly.
I knew it was for me
He said to drop my worries
And just live joyfully.

Take time to enjoy the simple things,
Like a new baby's cry.
All the beauty of this Earth.
The colours in the sky.

Take time to say I'm sorry.
Take time to help a friend.
Take time to share a smile.
Help a broken heart mend.

The past cannot be changed.
The future is unknown.
Now is all that matters.
Don't spend it all alone.

Barbara J. Hacking

Each day's truly a gift.
Meant to be filled with love.
"Thank you", I then whispered,
As he flew back up above.

I reflected on the words
That he shared so willingly.
What an amazing reminder
He had for you and me!

The ABC Islands

April 4, 2018

Visiting Aruba, Bonaire and Curacao had been on our bucket list for some time. During the fall of 2017, we finally made that happen.

In Bonaire, Mark and I were surprised to find milkweed when we accidentally took a wrong turn, while out exploring the Island. Mark had noticed a funny looking plant that resembled milkweed, although very different than any we had ever seen. It turned out that it was milkweed! It was loaded with caterpillars. The more we looked, the more we found. We felt like we had won a lottery. It's always a letdown when the Canadian Monarchs have flown to Mexico, so this was a real treat! Mark had fun educating Arnie and her friend, both from the Philippines, as well as other tourists who were curious about the Monarchs. We even found a milkweed plant that was two storeys high. I guess that is what happens in places where they don't have a cold winter season.

We visited a butterfly farm in Aruba and were delighted to see many tropical butterflies with colourful wings. A Swallowtail butterfly was madly laying her eggs and didn't mind an audience. We were curious to find out about the Monarchs that lived year round on their gorgeous island, as they have no reason to leave. The Blue Morpho Butterflies are one of my favourites. They are brown on the outside allowing them to camouflage themselves. They even have two spots that look like owl eyes that ward off predators. When they open up their large wings, the most beautiful blue iridescent colour is revealed. It is these wings that were used to create the framed picture that I was given as a child. I would have loved to have taken these butterflies home but knew that wouldn't be in their best interest, as there was snow waiting for us when we returned. I did have a hitchhiker that liked the red of my backpack.

We were amazed and felt right at home on these islands.

You Can't Jump Out of a Ferris Wheel to Fly with a Monarch! (If I Could Have...I Would Have!)

April 6, 2018

I woke up early this morning remembering a time when I took two young friends to Storybook Gardens. It was a perfect summer day and we were enjoying a ride up into the blue sky, dotted with whipped cream clouds, on the Ferris wheel.

Suddenly, I saw a colleague of mine way down on the ground, with her two young boys. Just as I waved at Cindy, a Monarch butterfly flew right past our seat. I couldn't believe my eyes, as Monarch sightings that summer (2015) were rare. If I could have, I would have jumped out of the seat to follow it. Cindy saw it too and captured it in the photo. I don't know what made me think of this! I checked Facebook and was able to find the photo which matched the picture I had in my memory bank. It wasn't just a dream!

Cindy Spendiff ▸ Barb Hacking
I thought it looked like Mrs. Hacking...then the
Monarch hovered by her so I KNEW it was her 😊

Looking Back at Retirement So Far

April 11, 2018

I was listening to a song as I exercised this morning. The words "Never let her wings touch the ground" stood out for some reason. That line stuck in my mind as I walked along the river and looked back over the last six years of my retirement from teaching.

It definitely has been a balancing act between being "too busy" and "too retired". At times, I have been extremely busy and have had to pull back on the reins and re-evaluate. Sometimes we need to let our wings touch the ground, even if it's for a short while, to refresh, so we are ready to go again.

My philosophy has been, if I don't like what I'm **doing** now that I'm retired, then it's my own fault.

As I was writing the word "doing" in the last paragraph, it dawned on me, that word was only one letter away from dying and the next stage after retirement, was just that!

Life is short and each new day is a gift…and a fresh start. It is important to shed the burdens of days gone by…find your passion that lifts your spirit high…be free to fly like a butterfly into the future….and whatever it holds.

Like the Monarch butterfly, which holds many mysteries…the future does too! And I wouldn't have it any other way.

Today's Challenge...Haiku

April 14, 2018

There was a challenge on Facebook this morning, to write a Haiku poem which is a three line, Japanese nature poem. I used to teach my students how to create them. For those children who had difficulty writing a lot, it gave them a wee break. Often the students would draw pictures on their poem and they were lovely impressions of the world around them.

As a Canadian spring ice storm was tapping at the window, I decided to give it a try.

Several attempts resulted in this.

Butterflies fly free...
Whispering their message.
Are we listening?

So simple. So true. So profound. So insightful...with very few words. I think I like Haiku!

There is an intricate balance that exists in nature. What does the declining Monarch population tell us? Are we listening to their messages? Are we doing our part to help them? What will their future be?

What will our future be?

Milkweed Magic

April 25, 2018

This year, I decided to try germinating some milkweed seeds. Attempts in the past have always resulted in failure.

In nature, these seeds would lay dormant under the snow. Therefore, it is important to give the seeds a period of cold temperatures.The seeds I collected last fall had been placed in our garage. You could also plant the seeds in pots or in the soil in the fall and leave them outside.

I carefully placed the seeds in a perlite/coconut shell mixture and waited patiently.

Finally, about a month later, I noticed one single plant popping up. The seed shell was still stuck to the green stem. I was so excited, however also disappointed that there was only one.

Today, when I checked it, I could see two leaves forming a heart. From the other direction I thought it looked like a butterfly. I must say, "I love my imagination!" A gift I surely received from my young students. It sure makes life fun and interesting.

April 26,2018

When I checked my milkweed this morning, what looked like a butterfly last night, now looked like a heart.

There goes my imagination again!

May 31, 2018

Eventually all of the seeds grew and filled my container. Now I am giving them away to people interested in helping the Monarchs. If you plant for them, they will come. Even one plant helps!

My Morning Inspiration

April 30, 2018

I woke up this morning thinking that education is the key to helping pollinators survive and thrive...but, it's much more than that.

It's being motivated and inspired to do something with that knowledge. For if one does not take action, there really is no change and the desired outcome is not achieved. I guess that holds true for many things in life.

When Bad Things Turn Into Good Things

April 30, 2018

I was saddened to learn on social media that the bee and butterfly house that was placed in the Ted Blowes Memorial Pollinator Peace Garden had been smashed by vandals. Luckily, the little tubules within the house that contained the mason bee cocoons were still intact.

With the help of social media, three people came forward to purchase new ones. So a not-so-nice situation resulted in two extra houses for the bees and other pollinators. This will provide them with a much needed habitat for the colder months.

Our city learned that if they painted beautiful pictures on the mailboxes around town, people stopped writing graffiti on them. Hopefully, the houses once painted by local school children will help people think twice about ruining them.

Often when we look on the bright side of a situation we can find positive outcomes. Sometimes, it may be the universe just steering us in a different direction.

Learning From Our Elders

May 3, 2018

I still feel one of the most unused resources in our world today are our elders. They are so full of knowledge, wisdom and history and enjoy sharing it with the younger generation, if asked.

Today I had the pleasure of speaking to a group of senior citizens about Monarch butterflies and other pollinators. When asked what they remember about Monarchs as children, they talk about seeing masses of Monarchs, especially at migration time. They remember seeing lots of different kinds of butterflies, too. Those were the days when pesticides weren't used and meadows were filled with wildflowers, including milkweed. Urban expansion into the rural areas has taken many of these habitats away. Wouldn't it be nice to see lots of pollinators in action again? Our food supply depends on them.

One lady remembered going out into the fields and collecting milkweed seed pods for the war effort during World War II. The fine white parachute attached to the seed, carries it to a new place away from the mother plant. This white floss was used to fill life preservers for airmen and sailors because it was light, waterproof and buoyant. Besides, synthetic fibers were not in use at that time. Time was of the essence during the war and to produce milkweed commercially would take three years. The government asked school children to contribute to the war effort by searching for the pods in the fall when the seeds were mature.

One day while out caterpillar hunting my friend, Luc and I stopped for lunch. Of course we couldn't leave our new found friends in the hot car so in they went with us. Sitting beside our table were Hugh and Joy. They were curious about the container and they became new found friends too. They had lived on a farm and recalled seeing many Monarchs long ago and how as children they were involved in the collection of Milkweed pods for the war. If they took an onion bag full of pods to the theatre they got into the matinee for free. That saved them a whole twelve cents. Now that's wonderful learning from pure human interaction. Probably not something found on the Internet.

I learn something new every day! Even about Monarchs and milkweed!

My mother-in-law once had a vase filled with meadow flowers, including milkweed. I chuckled as I asked her why she put milkweed in there. Was she trying to attract Monarchs in her kitchen? She chuckled back and asked, "Have you ever smelled their flowers?" I guess I hadn't! They have an exquisite scent similar to lilacs, when in bloom. Although I had been raising Monarchs for many years, I hadn't noticed.

Labour of Love

May 4, 2018 7:30 am

My dear, wise Mother always used to say, that something was a labour of love. I think I now know what she meant. I woke up this morning thinking that the writing of this book is more of an outpouring of love. The stories have flowed from my pen and it has never felt like a struggle. I love writing the old-fashioned way, with paper and a pen, which I believe is becoming a lost art. I never was sitting there trying to think of what to write. It was as if it came through me, not from me...until last night.

I had spent a couple of hours editing a story and revamping it on the computer. I had put it in the wrong place, so I highlighted it to move it....and lost it! Yes, all by the touch of the wrong button. It was a bit frustrating to say the least. This is the one time where I felt as though I laboured, tweaking this particular story and I thought I had it perfect.... but you know something? The second time around, it was even better! So although I was up until 2:00 am, it all worked out!

Oh, the joys of computers! When you handwrite something, at least it's still there. You can edit with just the stroke of a pen. I have since learned how to undo an action on the computer.

I must admit, using Google Docs when creating and editing this manuscript was absolutely ingenious. I was able to use my cell phone and my computer. Anything I added or changed on one piece of technology was immediately transferred to the other. I had a couple of grade four students explain Google Docs to me and I was off to the races. Technology truly is amazing! So are the children who seem to pick it up, as if it was second nature.

This experience reminded me to "Never force anything. If it's meant to be, it will be." When writing this story this morning, the thoughts flowed smoothly once again. Thank goodness

Living in Peace and Harmony

May 7, 2018

I stayed up until 3:00 a.m. working on getting my handwritten stories into a manuscript, on the computer. I am so close to the end! If the stories would just stop entering my head and circulating, until I am forced to write them down. Lots of energy was flowing, so I just went with the momentum that was being created. I used to do report cards this way and learned that when things were going smoothly to just keep on going, while the getting is good.

This morning I awoke to the sunlight streaming in the window. It took me back to that glorious moment on the mountains, when the Monarchs were dancing in the sun's rays, lifting up my spirits. The meadow was filled with millions of Monarchs demonstrating what it's like to live in peace and harmony. They share the air so peacefully and gracefully, never colliding or engaging in aggressive behaviour. I remember standing there in awe of their gentle souls. There are no words to describe the sound their many wings made, although it was music to my ears.

Each butterfly is beautiful and unique in their own way, yet they magnify each other's beauty, when interacting harmoniously, either in the air or huddled on the tree branches. Violence does not exist in their world and that is to be admired.

I find it intriguing how their messages are silent, yet profound if we choose to stop, watch, think and listen.

I finally am caught up. All of my stories written thus far are in my manuscript. I finished tonight at 9:00 pm. When I checked Facebook, I came across an author's challenge. The word author, now has a different meaning for me. I am now at the editing/publishing stage, so it's perfectly timed to remind me of my new identity. I guess now I can classify myself as an author. It's something that every medium I've ever seen has told me; that I had a book within me ready to be written. Had they just planted the seed that moved me in that direction? We will see what tomorrow brings.

This Never Ending Story

May 8, 2018

I think the stories have stopped. Perhaps I am really done after all!

May 9, 2018

Three more memories hit me today. I spent the day writing them.

The Real Ending

May 11, 2018

Five years ago today a very special man left this world! He was my mentor!...

Known as "Mr. Stratford", Ted Blowes always put others before himself. The project he was working on when he passed away is now complete. He wanted to create a memorial garden for those responsible for the peace we experience in Canada today. Little did we know, it would be part of The Ted Blowes Memorial Pollinator Peace Garden. The sign went up today to remind people that the peace they experience in a garden, came at a high price. My friend, Pauline Bokkers' photo of colourful blood-red poppies will serve as a year-round reminder of those brave souls we traditionally remember, only on November 11th.

Today, the milkweed shoots are just starting to poke their heads out of the sunshine-kissed soil, a signal that the Monarchs will soon be here. The milkweed plants will be ready to receive the Mama Monarchs' eggs and their flowers will nourish all the pollinators that love these plants. The garden will come alive with nectar-rich plants, educating those who visit about the importance of Monarch butterflies and all pollinators. We will be reminded of the cycles of nature and how man must protect this glorious world. Ted spent his days making our fine city beautiful, improving our environment and sharing his wisdom throughout the world, with his Communities in Bloom involvement.

So today, as I remember Ted, the writing for this book comes to an end. Who knows what Monarch magic will happen in the future? We will save that for the next book.

After the Real Ending

May 22, 2018

I just finished editing this book for the first time. The stories have stopped, finally!

When I was editing, I decided to number the stories. I couldn't believe it! 111! Now I knew for sure that the book was complete. 111, I believe is an angel number. My friend reminded me to check it out, on Google. I did and it all started to make sense. There are claims that the number 111 is a message from your angels or spirit guides and that your thoughts are manifesting into reality. Feel free to Google the meaning of 111 yourself.

I have always felt that I was being guided when writing, but by whom I do not know. My grandfather Eccles, was a poet. His son, my father, Sylvester Eccles was one as well. Maybe I just come by it honestly. I have this heartfelt gratitude to my silent partner(s) who ever he/she/they may be. Or, perhaps butterflies really do speak!

Now, I sit and wait! There are many open doors. One by one, they will close and I will know which one to walk through. You will know that I walked through one of these doors because you will have this book in your hands, or on your computer.

My Wish For You

June 28, 2018

Today as I place these final words in this book, I am reminded that yet another school year is almost finished. Six years have gone by so quickly since my retirement began. It seems right that I finish this book at this time of the year. As a teacher, I am used to the end of June being a time of finishing up and transitioning to something new. Even though I have tried to end the writing in this book many times, it now feels right.

Whether you believe these stories really happened or that I just have a vivid imagination, matters not. As Albert Einstein stated, "Imagination is more important than knowledge." He added, "Imagination is everything. It is the preview of life's coming attractions."

Louise Hay says, "Every thought we think is creating our future."

I hope that you will imagine the life that you want and thus manifest the life of your dreams. Our time here on Earth is too short to do otherwise.

It's now 1:11 a.m. on June 29, 2018. I just noticed that 2 and 9 in the date add up to eleven and so do the numbers in the year, 2018. Lots of 1's! There is a splendid full moon shining down upon the world and this book is officially done!

But is it??? I was walking along the Avon River admiring this tiny yellow bird, when I remembered two important things to add to the book. I stopped and added them to my notes on my phone so I would remember them, and the time was 1:11 pm.

July 18, 2018 (12:50 a.m.)

You will notice that there are a few more entries since I wrote the above. As I finish up again, a moth is dancing around the room. If it could talk, I'm sure it would be telling me to just push the button to the publisher. So my plan is to do that at 1:11 a.m.

Wishing you many butterfly blessings! Barb

A Final Note

June 29, 2018

I invite you to visit my Facebook page "When a Butterfly Speaks... Whispered Life Lessons" to see videos and more photos in colour. I would love to hear your butterfly stories there or at: barbutterfly7@ gmail.com.

This gigantic butterfly cloud filled the sky signaling to me that it was truly time to end this book.

Teach the Children Well...

Printed in the United States
By Bookmasters